# Raise your GAME NOW!

## With Paul 'Stalkie' Stalker

Editor – Dawn Leahey

With thanks to writers Jenni Hickson,
Bernice Walmsley and Chris Humphreys.

Sub-editor – John Clark

Cartoon ideas – John Random

Designed by Brilliant Ltd.

Published by V Beck Publishing Ltd.

V Beck Publishing Ltd.

F20 Allen House

The Maltings

Station Road

Sawbridgeworth

Hertfordshire

CM21 9JX

The website address is www.raiseyourgamenow.co.uk

First published by V Beck Publishing Ltd. 2006

British Library Cataloguing in Publication Data. A cataloguing record for
this book is available from the British Library.

ISBN 0-9553356-0-4

Typeset in ITC Officina Sans by www.brilliant.ltd.uk
Printed and bound in Great Britain by Bemrose Booth Ltd, Derby.

# Dedications

I'd like to thank my parents and sister; my mother for her unconditional love to date, my father for having unconditional faith in my ability and my sister for always being there for me.

My late grandfather Jack, for showing me how to have gratitude, the right attitude and to love the day.

My grandmother for never seeing anything but the good in me.

The officers of the 14th West Kent Battalion Boys Brigade for keeping me occupied as a young uncontrollable adolescent.

Nicola Stalker for blessing me with my four beautiful children Skye, Jack, Summer and Max.

My dear friends Julian Richer, Charles Dunstone, David Ross, Mike Blackburn and John McCarthy MBE, who have helped me so much in business.

All my colleagues at Paul Stalker Consulting, especially Dawn Leahey, for without her patience, care, kindness and wisdom, this book would not be here now.

# RAISE YOUR GAME NOW!

## Contents

# The Second Round:
# Gratitude and Attitude

# The Third Round: Make A Friend

## The Fourth Round: Enjoy Yourself

## The Final Round: Your Game Plan

# The Qualifying Round

## 1 My Story

### My Aim

**Hi! My name is Paul Stalker, aka 'Stalkie'.**

I am not one of those people born with a silver spoon in their mouth. I felt a failure at school, I've had cancer and a failed business - yes, life has not been so easy, but now...

I've beaten the cancer, made a million, learnt how to enjoy my work and built a life for myself that I love. My aim, my burning desire with this book, is to help you achieve your goals so that you get exactly what you want out of life, no matter what point you are starting from.

Using the methods and exercises that I will provide for you within this book, you will be able to transform your life. Whatever it is that you are searching for - a better job, a way to start your own business, the ability to overcome a health problem, to lose weight or stop smoking, to become wealthy, to find a partner in life or to make your relationship better with your partner - all these things are possible. After all I have been through, it is my mission in life to provide coherent strategies that support people so they are able to achieve their aim, whatever happens and whatever is thrown their way.

Now, I'm not telling you this is going to be easy. It requires both commitment and action. Anyone can read a book or attend a seminar but if they take no subsequent action, they will not change a thing. In this book, we'll look at ways in which you can overcome the inertia that can hold you back and stop you from achieving everything in life of which you are capable.

I have written this book using characters and events based on my real life experiences. Of course, the names have been changed, and the situations altered a little. The characters explain various points, so you can relate to real life challenges. Also, I have tried to use everyday problems that you can associate with in order to demonstrate how you can affect your own life positively.

## About Me

Now that you can understand where I am coming from and where my inspiration emerged from, I would like to share a few things that I have encountered in my life to date.

I didn't come from a wealthy family - quite the reverse in fact. My parents loved me, but didn't have the money to provide a privileged start in life for my sister and me. My biggest problem in my childhood - in common with so many people I speak to - was school. My teachers didn't quite understand me. Even more worryingly, they didn't understand how to motivate children or how to make them learn effectively. Consequently I was left with one of the biggest problems that I've had to overcome in my life - I didn't read or write very well.

### Schooldays

I vividly remember sitting in the classroom at school and, in the majority of lessons, being told to listen to the teacher or to read this, or write that; in truth, listening, reading and writing were things I simply couldn't do very well. I squirmed in my seat, and messed around doing nothing that would improve my performance. But, one lesson was different. It is still etched on my mind, as if it happened yesterday - it was a French lesson. We were learning how to say 'throw' and 'catch' the ball, and the young teacher made us actually throw and catch a real ball while saying the phrase, 'lancer le balle! attraper le balle!' What a brilliant idea! It was fun, and involved a new way of learning; what's more, it worked for me. If only that approach could have been expanded and applied to other subjects that I was hopeless at... well, who knows?

I felt misunderstood at school. If only my teachers had spoken to me, questioned me and found out what motivated me before using the information in an intelligent way to plan my learning, I could have been taught very successfully. I've certainly not had any difficulties over the last twenty years or so since I left school in learning things that were important to me, and interested me. The fact is, we do not all learn in the same way, and it would have been preferable if the teachers at school had tried to understand how I learnt, thereby uncovering the most effective form of teaching me as an individual. Unfortunately, this was not the case and there was a 'one size fits all' strategy at my school.

For example, there were two subjects at school that I adored and was good at; Sport and Cookery. There were two subjects that I hated; English and Maths. I never received any praise or encouragement from my teachers about my performance in Sport and Cookery. Instead, the time allocated for the subjects I excelled at was cut, to allow me to spend even more time doing what I was useless at! If only I had been able to progress in the subjects I loved, maybe I could have made a career out of them. Now, I'm sure many of you are identifying with my experience, and the solution is to do it yourself! It doesn't matter that your first try at education may have failed - try again! To start though, you need to discover your own motivating factors and your individual learning style.

Rather than grouping everyone together, it would have been great if my teachers had tried to gain an understanding of the way in which I learnt best. This, I am sure, would have helped me to succeed. They didn't seem to realise that everyone is different, and that people learn in different ways. Some people learn by assimilating information from books, some will learn from listening to their teacher and some will learn through more practical methods. Teaching must be tailored to the individual in order to achieve maximum success. We all have different strengths, and we must build on these in order to realise our potential. We'll look into how you can discover your strengths and make the most of them later in the book when we find out about the effects of positive psychology.

Another thing that surprises me when I look back on what I learned (or didn't learn) at school is that 'communication' was never mentioned, let alone taught as a subject - and yet, it affects every area of our lives. If we can't communicate effectively with our partners then our relationships will fail, if we don't communicate in business then we won't make a living or have satisfying careers, and if we can't communicate properly with doctors and other health professionals, asking the right questions in the right way, then we won't get the answers and treatment we need.

I was amazed to discover that this lack of emphasis on communication wasn't restricted to secondary education; indeed, I met up with a lawyer who told me that he'd never been taught how to use communication as a tool in his working life. This man, who makes his living - and a very good living it is too - out of communicating with clients, judges, witnesses, juries and colleagues has never been taught how to do it. Why not? This problem is not just limited to schoolkids and lawyers. It applies to nearly all other professions.

## Ambition

I felt immense frustration on leaving school at 15. I had a great desire to make something of myself, but didn't have the tools to achieve the right start in a career: no qualifications, no motivation, and no encouragement - I couldn't read and write properly, and I couldn't even cope with some of the practical subjects like metalwork. I'd always been told at school that I would never do well. My Mum did her best; she tried to get me into the Army, and when that failed, a training course with the local electricity board - all without success. She finally agreed to let me find my own job, whereupon I worked for MCA Music, struggling to operate a computer in the royalties department for a short while.

A major turning point came along when a friend bought me a gift; it was a series of motivational tapes by Dennis Waitley, entitled 'The Psychology of Winning'. Dr Waitley is considered to be one of America's most respected authors and speakers on high performance human achievement. For the last 25 years he has coached the likes of NASA astronauts, to Superbowl and Olympic champions; he's also helped individuals to personal and business excellence. In other words, he is inspiring.

These tapes were a revelation for me. At last, here was somebody talking in a language that I could understand. It enabled me to learn successfully for the first time in my life - and I enjoyed it! Not only did I understand what he was saying, I also felt moved by the content of those tapes. Dr Waitley talked about setting goals, thinking positively, believing in one's ability to achieve those goals and then going for them. I have no doubt those tapes provided a turning point in my life, and I am very grateful to the person who gave them to me. Over the years I really got to grips with what was being said on those tapes, and started to put some of what I was learning into practice.

At this time, I got a job with Exchange and Mart, selling advertising space. This was like a light switching on inside my head. I was amazed to discover that I could actually earn money, a lot of money, just by talking! It was a skill I already had, but nobody had mentioned it at school. I could talk to, and persuade, people - I found that communicating with complete strangers on the telephone held no fears for me. I had found my principal strength and I was in my element at last.

## Getting Motivated

During my time at Exchange and Mart I sold some advertising space to a car number plate dealer. Not long after, I asked whether I could go and work for him and he agreed to take me on. He helped me an awful lot and I soon had enough confidence to strike out on my own. I decided - at the tender age of 19 - that I could build my own business; my Dad lent me £200 (a lot of money to him at that time) to buy my first car, a Black Hillman Minx (thanks a million, Dad!). Actually, I didn't really want the car, just the number plate: 436 BAR. From there, I built up a business for myself. I had plenty of enthusiasm, and I'd learned about motivation and the importance of setting goals from listening to Dr Waitley's positive psychology tapes. However, I had no business skills.

I learned by making mistakes (NB: this isn't a good business approach!), and I took bad financial advice; hence, the business soon failed. I could buy, sell, motivate and communicate - but I didn't know how to run a business. No amount of positive thinking was going to get over my naivety in running a company. I learned some prudent lessons at this point that still hold true:

- Whatever you're doing - whether it's sport, fighting illness, raising a family, buying a house or running a business - good advice is absolutely paramount.
- You must understand that advice. Get a second opinion and some explanations. Keep asking questions until you understand.
- Get the right team around you in order to provide all the skills you lack (remember my reading and writing challenges?).

Being young, and taking on board these lessons, I bounced back from this failure and started another business. This time, I built up a publishing company. I still made errors, e.g. hiring staff on the basis of friendship instead of competence, and failing to learn enough about the numbers involved when it came to the financial side of things. But I must have done something right despite these shortcomings because, at the ripe old age of 28, I sold part of this business to venture capitalists and became a millionaire in the process - another goal realised. As with most businesses, there were still problems and I worked hard, cut costs and put myself under a great deal of stress. Although I didn't realise it at the time, my health and my relationships were suffering.

## My Health

I thought I had it all: I was earning good money, my wife was expecting our second child, I had a lovely home and a flashy car. On the surface, everything was going well and to everyone around me my life must have seemed charmed. But, I was working 12 - 14 hours a day and I hardly saw my wife, let alone our daughter. The time I did spend with my daughter was severely lacking in quality, because I was so tired I could have been anybody to her. The business became my sole focus, and I was paying the price in terms of health and family relations.

It was after a weekend away with friends and family that I discovered a lump on my neck. At first I put this down to carrying our daughter on my back in a harness, but it didn't go away. I went to an osteopath, because my back had begun to hurt as well; his advice was to see a doctor immediately. Meanwhile, the lump on my neck had become a bit of a joke in the office where it seemed I was living out the plot of the film 'How to Get Ahead in Advertising' in which an advertising executive is plagued by a talking boil on his neck! I tried to ignore it, but was eventually coaxed into an appointment with a GP by my sister and my PA.

At the surgery, the doctor examined me and said that he needed to refer me to a specialist. The following day I met one; he looked at me carefully and said "I think you've got cancer." It was said completely without feeling, and without compassion - totally cold. My sister Jo, who was accompanying me for support, burst into uncontrollable tears. The doctor showed no feeling when he spoke to me. He didn't try to explain himself; he didn't mention treatments, or what the next step might be. I felt as though he was treating me as just another number, nothing else. That doctor could certainly have done with a few lessons in communication!

The next nine days were the worst of my life. I was forced onto a treadmill of hospitals, tests and treatments - and I was unable to get off. I had a biopsy on the lump, a blood test and a CT scan (this involves injecting the body with a chemical to show up anomalies in the blood, as your whole body is passed through a tunnel-like scanner). At the end of those nine days my worst fears were realised.

The specialist told me I had Hodgkin's Disease. His words were mind-blowing, devastating, numbing - in fact, there probably isn't a word in the English language to adequately sum up the feelings that course through your mind and body when you're dealt those words. All I could say in reply was: "So, I'm going to die then?" The specialist said this wasn't necessarily the case. All I'd learned about how you respond to situations suddenly took on a completely different meaning. As Stephen Covey says in his book, 'The Seven Habits of Highly Effective People', you can be proactive and 'create perspective expanding experiences' by visualising situations that you might currently fear. I hadn't ever imagined that I would be in this position, but I was determined to find a positive take on this awful news. We'll learn more about the phenomenal effect that positive psychology can have on your health and other areas of your life later in the book. But, for now, consider this startling information that the Bristol Cancer Care Centre brought to my notice during my treatment:

At the Royal Marsden Hospital, they carried out an investigation into the beliefs of people who had been diagnosed with cancer. Beliefs included: 'I'm going to get over this', 'Maybe I can beat this', 'I hope I've got a chance' and 'I know I'm going to die, because I've got cancer'. Even though all of these people had the same disease, 80% of those who believed they were going to live, lived. In contrast, 80% of those who believed they were going to die, died. The difference positive psychology and belief can make when overcoming an illness is crucial, and this research proved as much.

## Fighting Back

Before all this happened to me I thought my diet was healthy enough, but now I started making an effort to treat my body with the respect it deserved. After all, if your body fails, where do you go from there? To that end, I started eating better food - less fast-food, more simply cooked fish and vegetables, more fruit. One night on my way home, I stopped off at a Chinese restaurant; instead of putting in my usual order, I explained my illness to the manager and asked if his chef would kindly steam me some fish and vegetables that I could eat with plain boiled rice. He agreed readily. Another hurdle was overcome.

Still on the treadmill of hospital appointments and different treatments, I started chemotherapy; but part way through the course I was told that my body was not responding in the way that they hoped. In plain English, the treatment wasn't working despite all the changes I'd made to my lifestyle and diet. This was yet another devastating blow. What now? Since listening to that first set of Dennis Waitley tapes, I had become a huge fan of other positive psychologists, motivational speakers, and those who study human excellence; these included Napoleon Hill ('Think and Grow Rich'), Steven Covey ('The Seven Habits of Highly Effective People') and Anthony Robbins ('Unleash the Power Within') all of whom had, and still have, a great influence on me. Now, their words took on a completely different perspective. If ever there was a time I needed the power of positive psychology, this was it. Their motivational writings were about to help me rebuild my life in a totally new way.

I thought I had taken my illness seriously enough, but that was proved to be quite wrong. The skills I'd learned from all those tapes, and the books I had read, were now put to good use as I began setting myself new goals. The specialist told me the reason my body was not responding to treatment

# "You only have six months to live — all of them Januaries."

was that I had poor quality blood.

Knowing I had to make even more changes, I set about discovering everything I could about cancer, diet and treatments. My inspirational friend Julian Richer, (owner of Richer Sounds, the company named in the Guinness Book of Records as having the highest sales per square foot of any retail outlet in the world, and author of 'The Richer Way'), prompted me to pay a visit to the Bristol Cancer Care Centre, where he was an advisor.

The Centre has a marvellous team of people working there, and a library full of books and videos containing everything one could possibly wish to know about the disease. I became convinced that juicing - taking fresh organic fruit and vegetables and squeezing the goodness out of them and into me - was the thing that could greatly improve my diet, and provide those benefits to my blood that I desperately needed. So, I started juicing with a vengeance. Every day.

As a quick illustration of just how powerful beliefs can be in affecting health, take this example: When my consultant observed the terrible toll chemotherapy was having on my body, he believed there was nothing more he could do. The general attitude was, 'that's it'. They thought I was going to die of this disease. After the initial shock, I started to become very thankful for life. I started making suggestions to myself along the lines of 'this is not going to happen'. Eventually, I wrote a plan of how I would beat it. I started by writing down exactly what I'd do on the first birthday of my then unborn son; I visualised being there with him, the cake, the presents, and all the friends and family who'd turn up to help us celebrate. I carried on this process by imagining all the things we could do together - when he was three years old, five years old, ten years old. I had to be there!

Through this process of visualisation, I created the reasons to try and get help with my life-threatening condition. This started sowing the seeds of belief and, as if by magic (although I now realise that it was my Reticular Activating System at work - more of which later in the book), I was activated to source doctors who thought differently from my original consultant. This was my catalyst for survival, and the start of my efforts to beat the disease. In this process, I had combined immense gratitude for the life I had with the belief that I was going to carry on living it and enlarge it. And it worked.

Through this mix of conventional and complementary medicine, the sheer hard work and self-belief on my part, and the support of my loved ones, I beat Hodgkin's Disease. By being proactive, and planning how I was going to beat the illness, I had succeeded. I was given the 'all clear' eight months after the weekend that I had carried my daughter on my back.

I was back in the game!

## Back In The Game

Beating cancer was a truly life-changing experience; it made me realise that the essential part of any business is the development of human potential. I was determined to spread the word about how we can all control and plan our lives, how we owe it to ourselves to look after our bodies and how we can all improve by learning communication skills.

I'd learned that communication is one of the fundamental keys to a happy and fulfilled life. Through communicating effectively with others, the riches this world has to offer will become apparent. And I don't mean riches solely in a monetary sense - the way we communicate, the way we behave with others that we come into contact with, will directly influence our quality of life. It will affect the way we feel about ourselves, our relationships, our work, our play and our legacies.

The years I had spent getting to grips with all those books (you'll remember that reading them had been a challenge in itself for me) were about to be put to good use. I decided that I must set up a new business that would give me the means to help people through passing on the life-changing lessons I had learned - and so I started Paul Stalker Consulting. In the last few years, I've enjoyed tremendous results working with some of the UK's leading companies, sports teams and successful individuals. I spread the word through my personal coaching, public speaking, live events and now, this book.

## This Is Just The Start...

As I said earlier, making changes to your life will not be easy. You can't just read the words of wisdom in this book and expect changes to take place. You need to do the exercises, find out about yourself and then take action. Think of yourself as a seed - a sunflower seed - with the potential to grow into an enormous, magnificent and beautiful flower.

To get from that tiny seed to the glorious bloom, standing many feet tall, the sunflower must be given the right conditions. It needs water, fertile ground and plenty of sunlight - lots of tender loving care. Your development needs the right conditions too. Building the life you desire is no quick fix. Think about the natural principles of farming; if you don't water the flower, it dies. There is no one-off quick action you can take - you can't water once and then go back in three weeks - you have to water every day. Of course, in the world of farming, if you don't look after a crop the disastrous end result is very visible, but with people it is not so obvious. Remember here that you must nurture your body and mind, without fail, forever, to produce the desired results. Your development needs to be farmed. If you try to break these natural principles, the principles will eventually have their way whether you like it or not.

Along the way, just like the sunflower, there will be many 'shoots' from your life. You may want to learn to drive, or play the piano. In order for these shoots to develop, you have to nurture them by practising. This means that you will have to add hard work, energy and training to the right conditions. Just like the sunflower, other seeds will come from your centre - your family, your  friends, your colleagues - and then the process will start all over again.

Now, I consider myself to be a lucky man, not only to have survived cancer but also to have finally found my true vocation in life. The series of events which have made up my life up to this point have lead me to believe absolutely in one simple truth: **You must plan your life and then take action**.

If you have problems in your life, or feel that you merely exist, you need to read this book and, working together, we'll Raise Your Game Now!

# The Qualifying Round

## 2 Why Raise Your Game Now!?

### Why 'Raise Your Game!' ?

**I would like to welcome you to the very first 'Raise Your Game Now!' book. Now you know a little about me and why I have written it, I would like to explain what 'Raise Your Game Now!' stands for and how you can get the best out of it.**

My aim is to take you on a journey. By reading this, you will discover where you are in your life at the moment and which parts of it need attention. This will be achieved by completing various exercises throughout the book, the results of which will help you gain the knowledge that you will need to build yourself into the person you desire to be.

The key elements that underpin this whole process are; **G**ratitude and **A**ttitude, **M**ake a Friend, and **E**njoy Yourself - or, for short, **G.A.M.E!**

### The Game Plan

Essentially, the outcome of this book will be your ability to realise your true potential. First you need to ask yourself a few questions: are you fulfilled in your life? Is your behaviour moving you towards your aspirations? Are you aware of the success, fulfilment and peace of mind that your job, your relationships and your family can bring you? How often do you think about your health? Statistics from the government show that one in two people will have heart disease, and one in three will get cancer. The most common complaint that doctors hear is lack of energy. In the main, all of these states can be put down to diet and lifestyle. Are you taking action, not only in terms of living life to the full, but through looking forward to watching your children's children grow up, and to celebrating your 100th birthday? Are you taking positive action to stop yourself becoming one of those statistics?

*Raise Your Game Now!* is about becoming what you want to be. If you gain the knowledge and then follow that with action, change will happen as a direct result. It is as simple as that!

## Where Are You?

Where are you now, and where do you want to be? How often do you sit down and spend time actually reviewing your life situation? Probably never - the fact is, we spend a lot of our time helping and planning for other people: our family, work, social events and sports teams. Where are you spending your time? Why not set aside half an hour at least each day just for you. Think about how many positive emotions you have in your life; are you moving towards these, or away from them? At what point are you willing to review your behaviour? How much pain are you willing to take in your life before you change?

It is time to start asking yourself these questions. How many times have you got into a situation, either in a job or a relationship, where you have found yourself trapped? Do you think 'I really don't enjoy this anymore', but stay in the rut because you don't have the motivation or the energy to get out of it? It may be a worn-out old phrase, but life really does pass you by. I want you to stop and think: What do I need to change?

# Why Take Notice Of Me?

I've had the pleasure of working with many different people; from those suffering with cancer and successfully conquering it, to a championship chasing polo team, to the racing crew of Enigma, who sailed for Great Britain in the Americas Cup. In the corporate world, I have worked with Charles Dunstone and David Ross, who run a well-known company called The Carphone Warehouse; with Julian Richer and his company Richer Sounds; with B&Q, with Woolworths and many others. These companies have utilised my skills to help create a cultural shift in the workplace. I try to get the best out of their staff by getting them enthused, and teaching them how they work as individuals. This results in a happier workforce, meaning happier customers and, as a by-product, sales increase, ultimately affecting the bottom line and profit. This has worked without fail. My company offers a 'money back' guarantee - that's how convinced I am that what I talk about works - nobody has ever asked for their refund.

This may all sound very impressive, but I believe that life is not all about how much money you have, or what position you are in - it is about you, because your life matters to you. It is the friends, family and the people you come into contact with that also matter.

My most rewarding moments have not been those where I've banked the biggest cheque, or won the biggest contract. They have been the times when individuals have come up to me after a seminar and said 'I have now got the courage to stop taking Prozac', and 'I have got the best relationship with my kids now after 20 years, thank you'. At one of my seminars, a female participant owned up to the fact she had always blamed her current situation on her father being an alcoholic. During the time she spent with me, this lady realised that she had to take responsibility for her own life, and not blame him at all. She now chooses her response to everything, and knows she can only change the future; the past is history. So can you - change the future, that is. You will discover the action you must take to regain control of your life when you learn how to 'Take the Power Back' later in this book.

My personal experiences described here in this book will help you become the person you deserve to be, and to create the life you want for yourself.

## Are You Up For It?

I sometimes have people say things to me like; "go on then - motivate me!" In truth, the only person who can motivate you <u>is you</u>. The minute you go to a restaurant expecting them to give you the best night of your life - the minute you go out with your friends and expect them to show you a good time - well, it just won't happen, because it's your responsibility. Put simply, life is what you make it.

Motivation comes in two forms: *Intrinsic* and *Extrinsic*. The first form of motivation is intrinsic motivation. Mother Teresa is a great example of this

"I just feel that life is passing me by."
"Vernon — you're a sponge. What did you expect?"

- she only wanted to help others because she cared deeply. There was no pay cheque or special bonus for her to save lives; she wanted to do it because it was in her soul.

Extrinsic motivation can be explained by looking at the example of the City trader. A City trader will not absorb the 24/7 pressure of working in a dealing room because they love it, or because it's good for their health - remember what happened to Nick Leeson, the 'rogue trader' who's misguided dealings in the financial markets lead to the collapse of his employer Barings Bank? Apart from a spell in jail, he also contracted cancer (from which, thankfully, he has recovered). No, a City trader will only stand the heat for thousands of pounds in return. This is *extrinsic* motivation - if the reward is not high enough, then the job won't be done.

If you only do something for a reward, you are extrinsically motivated; if you really want to do it because your heart is telling you it is right, then you are intrinsically motivated. Let's have a look at the different types of motivation in a little more detail.

## The Six Types of Motivation

There are six varieties of motivation and these can be grouped, as I explained above, into either intrinsic or extrinsic.

### Intrinsic Motivation

The first type of intrinsic motivation is *achievement by your own efforts*. This is typically where you work either towards a chosen professional qualification, e.g. you become a chartered accountant, or where you are self-taught in whatever trade you take up. The bottom line is that, through your own effort, competency, skill and attitude, you succeed.

The second type of intrinsic motivation is *the desire to be outstanding at what you do*. Maybe you will study John Gray's 'Men are from Mars, Women are from Venus' to really get the best out of your relationships? Maybe you want to be the best parent, and study accordingly? Do you genuinely strive for excellence? Is this a motivating factor for you?

## Extrinsic Motivation

The remaining types of motivation are all extrinsic. The third type of motivation is *the wish to gain status with experts* or with people you hold in high esteem - in other words, gaining recognition as a leader in your field.

The fourth type is *'thing' motivation*. Lots of people are highly motivated by 'things' and assets they buy, whether these happen to be cars, items of clothing or toys. Those motivated by material things are also more likely to want to keep the things they have, as well as to work harder on acquiring new things.

The fifth type of motivation is *the wish to gain status with colleagues, friends* and *family*. Do you want your colleagues to respect you because you are good at your job? Or your friends and family to admire your personal qualities? Is the question of how people perceive you a motivating factor in your life?

The final and sixth type is *the quest to win and to be number one, the big cheese*. How important is this to you? Do you have to be number one? Will you do anything to win? Sometimes, people cross the line to win at all costs and don't play fair. Others play within the rules and use this as the springboard to excellence.

## Where Do You Want To Be?

Now that we understand a bit more about motivation, we can look at how it might work for you. If you are in a leadership position, you will know how important motivation is, and you'll also realise that, for your colleagues to do a job well, they have got to want to do it. For you then, intrinsic motivation is key.

The qualities to look for when hiring your team are a person's desire to be outstanding, their drive for sheer exhilaration, and a hunger to test their limits. In a team member, you need to look for someone who wants to succeed and go to the top. Their individual standards must be geared towards excellence. If you combine this with the achievements of your own individual input, you will have the key to intrinsic motivation.

If a team member is more worried about the incentives they will receive for their services than their contribution to the firm, there is cause for concern. In essence, if your candidate is 'thing' motivated you should be wary. If they are not doing the job for the good of just doing it, when someone else comes along and offers bigger rewards, they will move on. If another company offered a car and a higher salary, they would take it. They would probably move again as soon as someone could offer them a better deal than that. If the candidate has a desire to be number one, be wary; there can only be one person at the top. If they got second place, would they stop trying?

Motivation is just as essential in your personal life. If you want to improve any areas of your life - perhaps you want to be a more caring friend, or to find a lasting relationship - then you must be motivated to put in the effort required. You are intrinsically motivated when you have a desire to improve, and to be the best. To make things better, we must learn continually.

Intrinsic motivation is the most important, both in business and our day-to-day lives. If you rely on extrinsic forms of motivation, and one day that external influence is not there, you won't be motivated. However, if you are motivated from the inside, then wherever you are, whatever you are doing, you will always be capable of rising to the occasion.

# Arthur Collins?

Within this book there are some complex psychological theories, condensed and simplified to make them easy for you to consume. I will do this by introducing you to the Collins family and their friends, who between them will illustrate that changing seemingly minor behaviour patterns can have tremendous and beneficial results.

I hope that you will be able to relate to at least one of the characters in this book. They have been created to put across salient points in a common sense format - many are based on real life individuals I have come across. You may read this book and think "well, that is all just common sense!" but you must remember, common sense is not always common practice. What you know in your head doesn't always become manifest in your behaviour.

I also want this book to be fun. Some people are very happy to sit and read long pieces of text; others find they have to ask a lot of questions when trying to understand a point, and some prefer to learn more actively, by doing exercises. Personally, I have difficulty concentrating on large chunks of text, and for this reason I have included cartoon illustrations and exercises ('Stalkie's Workouts') throughout to help those in the same position. Be sure to complete my Workouts, because they have been placed in the book very carefully to emphasise points. Do them with a friend, and have a laugh. The more you enjoy learning, the more it will stick with you long after you have put the book down.

Enough said. I would now like to introduce you to the Raise Your Game Now! characters:

# Meet the Collins Family And Their Friends

**Name:** Mr Arthur Collins **Age:** 45 **Work:** Full-time manager in a retail shop for a large company.

**Main Characteristics:** Arthur Collins feels that his way of doing things at work is correct, and that his employees should respect the fact. At home, the story is much the same; as a successful male, Arthur Collins feels that his wife should have a certain amount of respect for him and treat him accordingly.

**More Info:** Arthur Collins enjoys spending time with his best mate John, who is married, without children, and finds it hard to leave the house without his wife. As a result, Arthur tends to go out more with his single brother Ryan, who has no interest in settling down. Arthur Collins also has a sister called Patsy, who is married with one boy aged 6.

**Name:** Mrs Mary Collins **Age:** 44 **Work:** Mrs Collins works part-time as a teaching assistant at the local primary school; the rest of her time is spent looking after the family home and the children.

**Main Characteristics:** Mrs Collins feels as though her husband only ever thinks about his work, and does not understand her needs. She is sensitive and perceptive.

**More Info:** Patsy, Mr Collins' sister, gets on very well with Mary and relates to the problems she has with her husband. Frequent visitors to the Collins household include Mary's brother Jack, his wife Hannah and their two year-old twin boys. Jack and Hannah spend a lot of time with the Collins family, and share the baby-sitting.

**Name:** Kate Collins **Age:** 14 **Work:** Kate is the Collins' eldest daughter and goes to the local girls' school.
**Main Characteristics:** Kate enjoys seeing her friends and going shopping.
**More Info:** She is not very happy at her school. At home, she feels she does not enjoy the freedom she should have. Kate likes talking to Mrs Collins' best friend Jo who is single. Kate finds that she can relate to her far more than her mother or her aunt.

**Name:** Rachel Collins **Age:** 10. Rachel attends the school where her mother is a part-time teacher.
**Main Characteristics:** The Collins' younger daughter, Rachel loves school and shows great potential in various subjects. However, she really has a passion for sport, especially football and swimming.
**More Info:** Mrs Collins feels that Rachel's sporting interest may get in the way of her studies. Rachel enjoys playing with her twin cousins.

**Name:** James Collins **Age:** 6. James also attends the school where his mother works.
**Main Characteristics:** The Collins' only son, James is a happy boy both at school and home. He enjoys playing in the garden with Rachel at weekends.
**More Info:** James also likes playing with the twins when they come round.

**Name:** Ryan Collins **Age:** 36 **Work:** Ryan is a trained electrician who works on a freelance basis.
**Main Characteristics:** Ryan is single, with no interest in settling down. He is a huge football fan and loves going with his brother, Arthur, to watch their team play. Ryan is a smoker who wants to quit, but doesn't feel he has the strength to do it.
**More Info:** Ryan can be negative at times and he has a tendency to rely on others.

**Name:** Patsy Murphy **Age:** 38 **Work:** Patsy works full-time as the Personal Assistant to a successful company director.

**Main Characteristics:** Patsy can often blame others for the problems she feels she has, and she lets these problems get to her. She enjoys visiting her sister-in-law, Mary, for a coffee.

**More Info:** Patsy works very hard and doesn't get much time to spend with her husband, Simon, and her son. She often resents how much she has to do. Her relationships are suffering as a result.

**Name:** Simon Murphy **Age:** 40 **Work:** Simon works for a large banking corporation.

**Main Characteristics:** Simon is very good at his job, but he is a real family man and his significant others are the most important things in his life.

**More Info:** Simon wishes he could spend more time with his wife, Patsy, and their son.

**Name:** Jack Morton **Age:** 41 **Work:** Jack is a policeman.

**Main Characteristics:** Jack is quite a positive person who is always willing to learn new things. He enjoys spending time with his own family and also that of his sister, Mary.

**More Info:** Jack has always been content with his lifestyle - he has passed this on to his wife and children.

**Name:** Hannah Morton **Age:** 39 **Work:** Hannah is a Training Manager for a very large firm.

**Main Characteristics:** Hannah is a very confident mother, and always does the best for her two boys; however, she doesn't have the same confidence at work.

**More Info:** Hannah is a really proud mother - she regularly tells her children how wonderful they are, and how they make her very happy.

**Name:** Jo Middleton **Age:** 43 **Work:** Jo owns and runs her own hairdressing business.

**Main Characteristics:** Jo is a very upbeat and positive person, and she is a great friend to Mrs Collins. She also gets on very well with Kate, the elder Collins daughter.

**More Info:** Jo has always been a really energetic person, and she enjoys outdoor activities. She is a very loyal and happy individual.

**Name:** John Pierce **Age:** 46 **Work:** John is a freelance website designer

**Main Characteristics:** John enjoys spending time with Mr Collins, though unfortunately they don't get together as often as they would like to. John has spent a lot of time abroad, and loves telling the Collins family his stories.

**More Info:** Despite being good at telling stories, John has never had the motivation to become a writer.

## Take a Bite!

You can take anything from this book that will satisfy your needs; this can often work in surprising ways. I once worked with a colleague who, in many aspects of her life, was really stuck in a rut; one day I enquired what her favourite meal was, and she replied that she always ordered steak in a restaurant. I was curious at her use of the word 'always', so I asked if she ever ordered anything different, to which she replied 'no'. As our conversation continued, I discovered that her mother, with whom she lived, joined her in eating steak at every restaurant meal. I suggested that maybe she never tried anything new because she was following her mother's pattern. After giving it some thought, my colleague agreed with me, and decided it would be nice to try something new with an open mind! Now, she enjoys a variety of cuisine, and has applied this metaphor to the rest of her life. How true it is - if you never try, you will never know.

My colleague had never put her life in this perspective before. She never thought that maybe she was living her life to please her mother, rather than herself. While reading this book I want you to ask yourself; am I really becoming the person I want to be? I am not suggesting that you are going to agree with, and learn from, every point in this book; what I do suggest is that you look at this read as an opportunity, with each chapter constituting a new dining experience. Every page you read is like taking a bite, and only you will decide what works for you after you've digested it fully...

# The First Round
# *Getting Match Fit*

## 3 The Fear Factor

**We all have them; some of us deny them, others can't contain them, but whether we like it or not, emotions influence our lives. In order to Raise Your Game Now!, the primary emotion that I need you to understand and to harness is... fear.**

In extreme circumstances, fear can trigger changes in your body - accelerated heart rate, damp palms and forehead, acid in the stomach, a need for the loo - but it doesn't mean to say that you have to succumb to it.

Whatever your reasons for choosing to read this book, I would wager that the fear of change has been a significant factor in the passage of your life up until now. So, have you ever thought how you can work with fear to help you control your destiny?

## What is Fear?

The evolutionary theory of emotion suggests that fear has both positive and negative consequences regarding the way in which you focus your attention. Fear can govern your life in one of two ways. The first is that you react to it negatively by consistently visualising the negative pictures in your mind - this will prevent you from taking action. It adds to procrastination and, in many cases, is the catalyst for a downward spiral.

In contrast, the positive side means that you feel the fear in a situation but just go for it – you go for the job interview, you ask the girl/boy of your dreams out, you get married, you go for promotion, you get up on the stage and sing, you stand and speak in front of a crowd, you get strapped into the rollercoaster seat and so on - because you know that deep down, without going past your comfort zone, you will never grow and discover what life truly has in store for you. Individuals who react in this positive way towards fear often become addicted to the feelings associated with overcoming a difficult situation. Such people are often drawn towards taking part in extreme sports for example.

If you choose the negative response to fear, you may never achieve your desired result. Remember that only you are in control of your destiny. Which sort of individual are you going to become? Are you the sort of person who faces a fear so that, even though you are concerned, you listen to the signs and use them to your advantage, thereby becoming stronger for your next challenge? This can be described as *'stacking up your self-belief'*. On the other hand, are you the sort of person who just walks away from a fearful situation and thinks "it's all too much!", justifying to yourself why you haven't faced it. The choice is always yours.

Fear can present itself in many different situations. When John Pierce (a friend of The Collins Family) first came to England, he needed a job. He saw one advertised; it was exactly what he wanted. He thought about it again and again, and eventually picked up the phone. John dialled the number, but as the phone was ringing, he put the receiver down. His thoughts raced along the path of fear – "am I really what they want? I'm sure there is someone more qualified than me going for the job... will I really be able to take on the responsibility? Do I really have the skill set?" The fear became all-consuming for him, to the point where he couldn't think of anything else. After many restless days and nights, he decided not to apply. In the end, the totally irrational emotions that consumed his desires made him believe that he really wasn't good enough.

Look at the ratio of risk to reward in every situation. Going for a job has no downside, and no risk; if you don't get the job you are no worse off, but you have gained the experience of an interview, learnt how to improve your technique, and will think about how to present yourself better next time around. The conclusion is obvious: Why the fear? Experience only has an upside – there's no downside.

John's episode doesn't end there. The following week he woke up and, for some inexplicable reason, he thought "I've got nothing to lose. I'm going for it!" He called the number in the ad, only to be told that the vacancy had been filled. John politely asked for the details of the person who had got the job and was given the name of someone he knew - Phil. A red mist appeared as John was filled with anger, regret and sadness. He was so annoyed with himself that he started to really beat himself up, saying, "If only I had courage - why did I take so long to act? What's wrong with me? I know I could have done a better job than him. What's wrong with me? I'm just a loser. I don't deserve a good job if I can't even be bothered to ring in time." His negative thoughts went on and on.

In this scenario, John did actually 'raise his game'. He made the call – he really did do well. He could have said to himself, "Well done, John. You did it! You made the first move. A bit late, but I found the courage and did it. All I need to do now is remember my success so that, anytime I want to, I can do it again. I can apply for a new job - the world is my oyster." This positive affirmation would have been brilliant in the context of his next job application. What he should also be thinking is, "I did pick up the phone and call, but how could I do even better next time? Call quicker! That's what I have learnt." There is a very good chance that, by taking positives out of the experience, he would be so pleased with himself that he'd buy a newspaper and start calling the numbers in the job section straight away.

He was buried
alongside his career,
which died in 1990.

## Feeding It

After failing to get the job, John much later found himself in a very unpleasant situation. Whereas his initial phone call had been made on a whim rather than out of necessity, he now found himself being made redundant and out of work. Slowly but surely, John's savings diminished and he found it harder and harder to pay his bills until, eventually, the opportunity to work in the same company as Phil - albeit in a much lesser position - arose. To avoid the pain of hitting rock bottom and losing his house, John went for the interview and subsequently took the job. Now, John watched from afar as Phil got promoted and moved up the company; he still consistently thought that he could have done a far better job than Phil, and now it was even more painful to bear.

Each time John thought about Phil, negative feelings came flooding into his body - and he let these feelings remain, instead of 'taking the power back' (a concept that we shall explore more in The Second Round of this book). Knowing it was his own fault that he hadn't organised that first interview with the company made John feel remorse, hate and anger, not against himself but against his poor unsuspecting colleague, Phil.

John remained in his lowly position for years, whilst Phil climbed the career ladder. As a result of his bitterness, John started to gossip about Phil, saying how bad he was at the job and desperately trying to tear him down. As time went on, John developed a blame mentality towards the company and other colleagues for his lack of career progression. He never tried to take the power back and pro-actively seek a better position, or a job elsewhere. Instead, he stayed in the same role, getting his needs met in a negative fashion by gaining affection and connection with the colleagues he gossips with. These people also provide him with a feeling of significance and variety in his boring day-to-day existence, because their own negative attitude makes them gravitate towards John.

Many people hold themselves back in their lives because of fear. Often, they don't actually realise it because they're too busy convincing themselves how bad their partner, boss, company or friends are. They think "it's not me - it's the others", whereas in reality it is they who have the problem, because they are not facing up to a particular fear. Moreover, they're not big enough to admit that to themselves. Are you one of these people? If so, you will never be truly fulfilled – unless you deal with it.

## Facing It

Will is an old friend of Mary Collins. He went into a bar with some friends for a few Friday night drinks - the place began to fill up and the atmosphere grew, setting the lads up for a really good night. Then, Will spotted Julia and remarked to one of his friends; "Have you seen her over there? She is gorgeous! I'd love to speak to her". "Well, what's stopping you?" came the reply.

Fear could have stopped Will. The fear of rejection, in fact. What if she ignored him? What if she laughed in his face? What if she didn't fancy him? What if his friends thought it was a laugh and made fun of him forever more? She may even take the Mickey out of him and say "I wouldn't go out with you if you were the last man in here."

However, you can transform this fear of rejection into enthusiasm and connection, because *fear can be turned into power*. Instead of shying away, Will used the power of focus and thought about their first kiss, walking hand in hand, and dancing and laughing together. Thus, he used the correct physiology, puffed his chest out and walked over to Julia in a determined manner, constantly affirming to himself that she was going to say yes to a chat and a dance. The Triangle of Communication (more of which in The Second Round) really worked for Will; he got just the answer he wanted. He danced and chatted with Julia all night and now, he and Julia have been together for a year. Of course, Will was nervous of rejection, but he couldn't face having to think about what might have happened. For Will, the pain of not knowing would have been bigger than the rejection itself.

When you find yourself in a challenging situation, what do you do? This depends on how you deal with your feeling of fear. Will chose to use his as an asset rather than a liability - he used his confidence to speak to Julia with passion, fun and persistence. It is true that he might have been rejected, but he could still have taken the positives out of that situation; looking at the risk to reward ratio, if she turned him down then he would still be one rejection closer to a 'yes'. He would have been no worse off, because he didn't have a girlfriend at that time anyway. If it had all gone wrong, he could have learnt what not to say, refined his chat-up lines and tried a different approach on the next lucky lady. When Will thought like this he psyched himself up, took a quick swig of beer and went over to the girl. As a result, he doesn't have any of those 'what if?' feelings that can eat away at you for days, months, or even years afterwards.

## Dealing With Fear

Do you listen to your emotions, and also your fears? Do you think of fear as your enemy, like John, or do you let it help you, like Will? Whatever your fear, it can be controlled, and used to your advantage. Fear is an incredibly strong emotion, and everyone deals with it in very different ways, including the following:

### A. Avoiding It

Jack and Hannah's best friends Sue and Trevor were having problems with their marriage. They both knew that they had problems, and that things were not working in their marriage like they used to. However, neither of them wanted to even think about separation, because they were fearful of losing each other, being rejected by others, hurting the feelings of others, the great unknown, and being on their own. They only focused on the negatives of separating.

What Sue and Trevor could have done is agree to talk about the situation until they really understood each other – and, they might have agreed to keep talking until they came up with a solution, or trial, they both felt happy with. To try and make a go of their marriage, they needed to focus on the positives - how they were when they first met each other, how they once couldn't be separated from each other, how they laughed together. But, Sue and Trevor chose to avoid their fears, and carried on acting like single people who just happened to be living under the same roof.

As a result of their fear avoidance, Trevor and Sue simply co-existed, never really experiencing the love or wonderful times they had previously enjoyed as a new couple. When it came to meeting each other's six basic human needs (more of which in The Third Round of this book), Trevor no longer helped Sue meet her requirements for love and connection, contribution and significance or importance, and so she had a void in her life. Before they started to have problems, Trevor had been the vehicle that provided these needs. Now, Sue just concentrated on her children and became an overbearing mother, because she needed to be loved, to feel important and to contribute to someone or something. Because she wasn't having any of her needs met by Trevor, Sue would try and manipulate situations so that her children would show her more love. The children were growing up, but Sue insisted on telling them what to do and how to do it because she had to contribute and feel needed, even though her input wasn't required most of the time. By contributing, Sue tried to make herself feel important.

Trevor chose other routes to meet his needs. First of all, it was his career; he threw himself into his work, because he knew that would help him to meet his needs for significance / importance, love and connection, growth, and contribution. As a result, Trevor spent so much time in the office that his relationship with Sue deteriorated to the point where he actually found love at work, and started an affair with a colleague.

## B. Ignoring It
Some people don't even bother to avoid their feelings - they simply ignore them. This is most definitely a worse option.

"It's no use, Angela.
I don't feel my emotional needs
are being met."

After many months of discontent, Trevor and Sue (who continued to live together) hit a new low in their relationship because they continued to ignore their fears, whilst their marriage just followed the route of a downward spiral. People will often only act when they are trying to avoid pain or gain pleasure, i.e. the pain becomes too much to bear or the pleasure is too good to miss out on. Trevor, after finding love again and wanting the good feeling even more, began to avoid pain, and was thus motivated to act. He'd hit breaking point, and filed for divorce.

### C. Starting a Competition With It

Another thing Sue did was to compete with her friends. They would all meet at the local gym, have a swim and then do lunch, whereupon they would share stories about how bad things were for each of them at home. They would get into a real blame culture, discussing how the children were not doing this or the husbands were not doing that; sometimes, one of them would mention something negative about her husband or children, and the others would then come up with "well, if you thinks that's bad, listen to what's happened to me!" stories. This behaviour solves nothing, and simply reveals that others are just as unhappy as you. So, if you intend to die having lived an unhappy life, just remember – you're not alone!

### D. Listening to It

Will is a good example here, because he felt the fear in a situation but faced it anyway. He looked at the risk to reward ratio, and raised his game. Are you going to raise your game and dance with your fear? **Redirect your fear into power to make changes in your mind, body and soul.**

### E. Regretting It

Next, we move on to those people who live with their regrets. They justify why they didn't face their fear by saying that the job, person, situation etc. was silly – "all men are selfish, boring and egotistical" and "the job isn't worth having anyway" is the sort of thing you might hear them say.

If you let bad situations continue – just as Sue and Trevor did with their marriage - you may end up with constant feelings of regret. It's a very difficult emotion to live with. If you've ever felt annoyed or upset with yourself for not making the most of your opportunities, you will know how infuriating, saddening and even depressing this can be. Moreover, if you are fearful of applying for that dream job, sorting out your relationship with your partner or trying something new, you could feel regret because you will have just existed, instead of living life to the full. You will never know whether you have reached your full potential. This is the result when you choose to ignore or deny your feelings and emotions, and it's especially true if you deny the emotion of fear - there will be repercussions every time.

***Raise Your Game Now!***
*Make the most of your opportunities; don't live with regret.*



## F. Using It!

Where fear is concerned, the best approach is to use it to your advantage. Turn it into power! You will be faced by fear in your everyday experiences; but you must stand strong. Always think of past glories; recall a time when you managed to overcome a difficulty, and focus on that. If you are faced with fear, you kick into 'fight or flight' mode - your body will assess the situation before telling you to either fight the fear, or run away from it. If you choose to ignore the fear altogether, then you will never gain anything from it. So, when you feel fear, and get those butterflies in your stomach, you must devise the best strategy for surviving the situation. Amazingly, fear can enhance your life.

## Stalkie's Workout

*When you feel fear or apprehension, you may like to use this exercise whilst thinking of the best strategy to confront and overcome it.*

- *Close your eyes.*
- *Breathe normally.*
- *Take one deep breath in, and imagine that all the anxiety is now in your lungs; as you exhale, you are blowing it out of your body.*
- *Repeat this exercise until all anxiety has been removed from your body.*

# Understanding Fear and Befriending It

**How does fear manifest itself?** Nervousness, anxiety, apprehension.

**How does fear show itself in our minds and bodies?** Poor sleep, loss of appetite, sweats, heart beats faster, lack of focus, sweaty palms, short tempered, nervous energy, acid stomach.

**What causes fear?** The known/unknown, a threat to safety, being unprepared, new situations.

**What can we do?** Accept fear as normal, welcome fear and go with it, treat it as a motivator, know you are learning from every situation, use it as a tool for improvement.

Practical steps - visualise the positive end result, practise visualisation, see yourself winning, use relaxation techniques, accept and welcome fear as another helpful feeling.

*Raise Your Game Now!*
*Pain is only temporary, regret is permanent.*

When you are sitting by the fire in your twilight years, you won't want to regret the things you didn't do as a result of fear. By that time, it will be too late...

Raise your GAME Now!

# The First Round
## *Getting Match Fit*

### 4 The Health Factor

**How often do you service your car? Would you ever consider driving your car for 50,000 miles or more until, when you start it up in the morning, there is a big grinding noise coming from under the bonnet and large clouds of smoke billowing from the rear? You have to look after your car, otherwise it will not work properly.**

Do you regularly service your body? Just like a car, your body needs to be serviced. You need to give it the correct fuel (water and nutrition), exercise, and take time out to relax. If you don't put fuel in a car, then it won't start. If you never drive your car, it will be difficult to start when you want it to. On the other hand if you never give your car a rest, it will eventually stop working. The same is true for your body.

## Taking Care of Yourself

People are really good when it comes to taking care of cars, houses and families but where looking after number one is concerned, they take short cuts. Do you make sure you have three or four meals a day? Do you drink enough water? Do you take regular exercise? In the modern world, everyone is guilty of skipping meals or not bothering to exercise. As a result, society is becoming sick.

People tend to skip breakfast, have a couple of coffees, a quick lunch and then a curry for dinner with a few beers. They go to bed late and wake up feeling tired. This can become a repetitive cycle, and often results in a necessary trip to the doctor's surgery.

Ryan believes that drinking a couple of beers a day won't hurt. He enjoys spending time at his local pub and going out for a kebab afterwards. Most of Ryan's friends are the same; they all love a lad's night out. One of Ryan's colleagues, George, often sees the results of Ryan's nights 'on the town'; he's always trying to encourage Ryan to look after himself.

"Ryan, did you know that one in two people in the Western world die of heart disease?"

"No, I didn't know that George!"

"Ryan, did you know one in three die of cancer?"

"No George, I didn't know that!"

"Ryan, take me seriously. Suppose I said that, if everyone managed their finances in a certain way, one in every two people will end up bankrupt - would you follow suit with your money?"

"Course not!"

"So why do it to your body?"

"I don't know mate, I don't really think about it. It's just one of those things; when your time is up, it's up. What's the point of worrying? I could get run over by a bus tomorrow. I enjoy what I do and what I eat, so why should I stop?"

Both cancer and heart disease are over 75% lifestyle related, and one in three hospital admissions are alcohol, smoking or obesity-related. This means that, once we all get proactive and look after our bodies, as much as three-quarters of what we spend on healthcare could go towards enriching our lives instead. Just think about all the suffering and heartbreak that could be saved too. It's really quite simple – we must all take the decision TODAY to become proactive and treat our bodies like the precision instruments they are.

# The Value of Good Health

Ryan's attitude is the same one that many people have – but what is this
costing the health service and the general state of the country? The
government spends approximately £90 billion per annum on sickness,
healthcare and disability (Source: Office for National Statistics 2000/1). If
we saved three quarters of this, they would have in excess of £67 billion
each and every year for education, or improving healthcare for the
remaining sick people. All this could happen if everybody just took care of
themselves.

No doubt you will have read or heard somewhere that you should cut
down on fatty foods, drink less alcohol, quit smoking and do more exercise.
The messages are out there. It's on television all the time, while magazines
and newspapers carry advertisements for new slimming products such as
biscuit bars with 50% less fat. There are plenty of low-fat meals in
supermarkets, and TV programmes like 'Fat Families', 'Jamie Oliver's School
Dinners' and 'You Are What You Eat' appear all the time. New slimming clubs
and magazines aimed at improving your health or reducing your weight are
being launched on a regular basis, and 'stay fit at your local gym' is
constantly being advertised too. Your health, and that of your family, is
vital! You are aware of all this, but what are you doing about it?

Arthur Collins is a fairly typical businessman, in that he believes his way
is the best way at work; he also thinks that when at home, he should be
treated as the man of the house. Arthur does very little exercise, and
adores being served a full English breakfast in the morning, plus a hearty
meal in the evening. The truth of the matter is, if Arthur continues to eat
his high-fat, high-carbohydrate diet and hardly exercises, he could become
seriously ill. Actually, a lot of people are making themselves unwell through
the lifestyles they lead – just like Arthur.

It's more than likely that you have at least a vague understanding of what you should and shouldn't eat and drink, but at the same time you're probably guilty of doing exactly the opposite. Mr Collins has read somewhere that he should drink two litres of water a day, but he can't find the time to actually do this. He is also aware of the government's guidelines on eating five portions of fruit or veg a day – but the thought of tucking into fresh fruit salad in the morning rather than two fried eggs and bacon is just too much for him. Like so many other people, Mr Collins' waistband is tightening, and he can't run for a train or bus without breaking into a sweat and gasping for air.

## Physical Health, Mental Wealth

Your body, just like your mind, needs stimulating and nurturing in order that it can grow and perform successfully. Health is defined by the World Health Organisation as being 'soundness of body', but it is also energy, zest for life, enthusiasm, keenness and 'get up and go'. Without good health, the rest of your life could suffer – the state of your body affects everything you do, including how long you are able to concentrate, your behavioural patterns, your ability to cope with pressure and the amount of energy levels you have for the day.

If you've any remaining doubts about the value of eating well, look at two situations that have been in the news recently; school dinners, and the film 'Supersize Me':

The celebrity chef Jamie Oliver started a campaign to improve school dinners, and was appalled at the observations of a south London doctor who said he saw many children who were so badly constipated because of the poor quality of their diet that they had actually started to vomit their own faeces.

With the right food at lunchtime, teachers have noticed an upturn in concentration and general health levels. A London head teacher commented: "Children who are hungry and eating highly unsuitable things are bound to behave badly." He's also noticed that, whereas before a huge number of children needed asthma pumps, far fewer now do.

In his film 'Supersize Me', Morgan Spurlock undertook to eat nothing except McDonald's meals for a month. The results were staggering. Not only did he feel and look awful, but doctors who were monitoring his progress found that his liver was on the verge of collapse after just a matter of 2 - 3 weeks – and they begged him to stop. His partner also reported a detrimental effect on their love life.

The word 'breakfast' quite literally means to 'break your fast'. Mr Collins really does enjoy his full English breakfast: Eggs, bacon, sausage, beans, mushrooms and fried bread, all washed down with a cup of tea. Why do so many people have this type of breakfast? It is down to social conditioning – you learn to eat like this. It's the same with an evening meal consisting

Supersize me –
the birth of a concept.

of a starter, steak and chips, ice cream, cheese, and bread and butter, sent down with wine, beer, liqueur and a few chocolates to follow. Here, we get a full day's calories in one sitting whilst sending our systems into complete toxic overload. Fruit and vegetables, the vital live nutrients that we need to get our motors running, are absent. It's just not an effective way of feeding your body.

## Our Vital Elements

In order to achieve optimum health, we all need:

### Cells

Every living thing - whether man or woman, lion or tiger, tomato plant or rose - is made up of cells. In the average human body there are approximately 75 to 100 trillion cells, and they all need to be kept healthy.

What makes some people more enthusiastic and energetic than others? The answer is in our cells. To understand how you work, you need to understand cells - so take a look here at the photos of some blood cells.

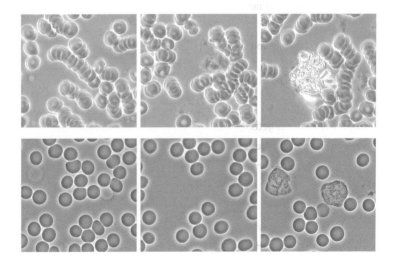

The top row of photos reveals what unhealthy blood cells look like under a microscope. These were shown to me at The Diagnostic Clinic in London where I go every year now for a health screen. The practitioners evaluate my level of health and fitness and prescribe supplements and exercise for any areas that they feel are in need of improvement.

Unhealthy blood cells may show up as irregular in shape or spikey looking, or can be seen stuck together in long chains. The spikey cells are called acanthocytes and the presence of these in the blood indicates possible free radical damage and nutritional deficiency states. Blood cells that are stuck together in long chains are generally indicative of dehydration or free radical activity. Free radicals are negatively charged particles that can damage arterial vessels and cause cellular changes. The principal causes of free radicals are toxins, pollutants, fried foods, lack of exercise and stress.

I will be explaining as we go along some of the simple things that can be incorporated into anyone's lifestyle, the results of which can change unhealthy looking blood cells into the healthy looking blood cells you can see in the bottom row of photos. Remarkable isn't it, to look inside the body and see how good nutrition and exercise effects the very cells themselves?

To keep cells healthy you need to provide them with many things, so let's look at how this is done:

## Oxygen

A major key to life is getting oxygen into your body. You do this by simply breathing in and out. You breathe in oxygen, and its energy is then coupled with a complex molecule called Adenosine Triphosphate (ATP). ATP is a little powerhouse molecule that transfers high-energy bonds from nutrients into the energy needed to run our bodies.

Ryan, Mr Collins' brother, loves his car; he believes his little MG is a living, breathing thing. He isn't far wrong. The MG needs oil and water, just as your body needs nutrients and water. Your ATP molecule is like the engine of the MG, which takes in the oil, water and petrol and then converts them into energy so that the car can work. ATP, our engine, takes in the nutrients and water, and harnesses the energy from healthy, live foods, so that work can be carried out effectively in our cells.

## Effective Nutrition

As well as needing oxygen, your body also requires healthy food; you need to give your body maximum nutrition. It is absolutely worth knowing how good nutrition can help in keeping you healthy. The health of your body is under your control, and all you have to do is start giving yourself first-class, healthy food that's high in vital energy and all the vitamins, minerals and nutrients you need. My health expert, Dr Rosy Daniel, has now worked for 20 years to help people with serious cancer fight back from the brink. The mainstay of her recovery plan is healthy eating, with plenty of vegetable juices; the following represents her simple guidelines for a top-class, healthy body.

## How To Eat Yourself Healthy

In essence, to be healthy you need to eat meals that are rich in fruit, vegetables, pulses and grains; they should be low in animal fats, animal protein, sugar, additives and refined foods. To take the path to a super-healthy body:

1 Eat non-acid fruit and vegetables at every single meal. Include a high proportion of raw fruit and vegetables every day, either on their own, in salads or via homemade vegetable juices - these represent an excellent source of nutrition. Get yourself a juice extractor, or better still use a juice press.

**2** Replace refined and processed foods with the whole food, unprocessed equivalent. This means replacing:

- White bread with brown bread
- White rice with brown rice
- White pasta with brown pasta
- Ordinary cheese biscuits with oatcakes
- Sugary cakes with fruit cakes
- Processed breakfast cereal with muesli or porridge
- Sweets and chocolate with nuts, dried fruits or fresh fruit
- Sweetened drinks with mineral water, or homemade juices

**3** Replace intensively-farmed red meat, chicken and fish with vegetable protein from beans, lentils, peas and quinoa. Go the vegan route if you can, but if this is not realistic, supplement your diet with occasional organic, wild, deep-sea fish, salmon or trout, free-range organic chicken and game, free-range organic eggs and very occasionally organic red meat. Introduce as much variety into your diet as possible, and try different pulses so that you get a full spectrum of minerals and vitamins.

**4** Replace animal fats with vegetarian equivalents. The exception to this rule is fish oils, which are helpful because they contain essential omega 3 fatty acids. These are found in oily fish such as mackerel, herrings and salmon (organic), and you can also take fish oil tablets. Otherwise:

- Replace your regular milk with skimmed milk or, better still, vegetable milks such as Soya, oat or rice milk. Try to cut dairy milk from your diet altogether by drinking tea weak and black, and using fruit juices on muesli for breakfast. Porridge can be eaten without milk - instead, flavour it with fruit concentrates, or date/maple syrup.

- Replace cheese with vegetable pâtés, such as olive, aubergine, avocado (guacamole) and mushroom. It is also better to use a fish pâté than cheese. However, you should check that pâtés or pastes are not full of 'hidden' cream cheese.
- Replace animal cooking fat with vegetable oils - preferably cold-pressed olive oil or ground nut oil. Use speciality oils for flavouring salad dressings, e.g. sesame oil and walnut oil.
- Replace your normal cream with Soya cream, ice cream with Soya ice cream, dairy yoghurts with Soya desserts (such as Provamel), and butter with vegetable equivalents such as olive oil based spreads or margarines which do not contain hydrogenated fatty acids (like Vitaquel and Granose).

## The Importance of Being Alkaline

The biggest health news of the moment is this: most of our degenerative diseases in the West, like cancer, heart disease and arthritis, are being caused by having bodies which are too acidic. Foods, drinks and behaviour which acidify the body are:

- Acidic drinks such as wine, fruit juice, fruit teas, tea and coffee, fizzy drinks, fruit cordials.
- Acidic fruits such as berries, and citrus fruits, e.g. lemons, oranges, grapefruits, pineapples, apples, grapes and other soft fruits. If you do eat fruit, ensure that it's as ripe as possible because that will make it less acidic.
- Yoghurt
- Pickles
- Vinegar
- Berry jams
- Excess protein from meat, fish and shellfish
- Smoking

- Lack of exercise
- Shallow breathing or breath-holding if you are anxious

So, the best way to get the body alkaline is to eat a vegetarian diet based on:

- All vegetables except tomatoes
- All pulses, nuts, seeds, grains and cereals
- Non-acid fruits such as melon, banana, papaya, dates, figs and sharan fruit
- Fresh filtered water, herb and green teas, and vegetable juices
- No more than four ounces (120 grams) of protein in any one day

## 'Acid-Forming' and 'Alkaline-Forming' Foods

Confusion is created by lists of foods that are acid-forming and alkaline-forming. For example lemon, clearly an acidic fruit, is an alkaline-forming food because when eaten, the body buffers its acid with alkali. In order to do this, alkaline buffers are used up and as a result, the tissues become progressively more acidic. Lists of these foods will therefore tend to be back to front! For this reason, it is vital to eliminate food and drink types that are acidic themselves, rather than being acid-forming.

Your body is consistently trying to maintain an alkaline balance. Your cells work very hard to keep you healthy, but if you are too acidic you will become ill.

## The Litmus Test

The pH (acidity) of your body, plus the food and drink you may be taking, can be tested with litmus paper. Check your salivary and urinary pH twice weekly to assess your body's status. This should be done first thing in the morning before drinking, eating or brushing your teeth. It can be helpful to keep a chart, because this will enable you to notice the change as you eliminate acidic foods.

Litmus paper is available from our health partner, Health Creation on 0845 009 3366 at a cost of £10.00 per roll. You are aiming for a salivary pH of 7.5 (which is on the blue side of neutral on the litmus paper dial). Results less than 7 are acid, and you have work to do immediately to get the body alkaline.

## Your Healthy Shopping List

To get truly match fit, your food cupboard and fridge should consist of:

### Grains

- Brown rice
- Cous cous
- Quinoa (a great source of protein)

### Soya Products

- Tamari soy sauce for flavouring
- Tofu or bean curd (a great meat substitute in Chinese restaurants)
- Silken tofu
- Soya milk
- Soya margarine
- Soya meat substitutes, i.e. Soya mince, sausages and even 'meat' pies - check out the Linda McCartney range

### Beans & Pulses

- Chick peas
- Red kidney beans
- Lentils
- Butter beans

### Dried Fruit

- Dates
- Apricots
- Figs

## Organic Fruit & Veg For Juice Making

- Carrots
- Beetroot
- Celery
- Melon
- Ginger - for flavour if you like it hot!

## Oils

- Olive oil
- Linseed oil
- Toasted sesame oil

## Honey and Syrups

- Local honey
- Date syrup
- Maple syrup

## Cereals

- Wholewheat flour
- Muesli
- Porridge oats

## Pasta

- Wholewheat spaghetti or shells

## Seeds

- Sunflower seeds
- Sesame seeds
- Pumpkin seeds – good for your sex drive, too!

## Nuts

- Walnuts
- Brazil
- Peanuts
- Almonds
- Cashew
- Pistachio

# Learn to Love Water

The earth is made up of approximately 70% water and 30% mass. Strangely, your body closely mirrors these proportions, being 80% water. Therefore, you need to make sure that you have a large intake of really good quality, filtered water. Whenever you become ill, the first thing you're told is to make sure you drink lots of water, so that all the toxins which have built up in your body overnight, from the chemical processes of the body, can be flushed out of the tissues.

# Keep it Live

In addition to the above, it is vital that we eat what is called 'live food'. This is food which has not had the life cooked, microwaved, processed, fried, irradiated, frozen or chemically taken out of it. Foods in this category include fresh vegetables, fruits, salads, nuts and seeds, plus fresh cereals and grains; all of them contain a large amount of living enzymes and nutrient substances called 'phyto-nutrients'. In nature, these substances can actually reverse the formation of cancer cells - but only if they are still alive. All such substances are very sensitive to heat, cold and irradiation, not to mention many of the other processes by which food is processed and chemically treated to keep it fresh and looking perfect for the supermarket shelves. When altered too much, the good things in these foods effectively die, and therefore become useless at protecting us from cancer and heart disease. So, you must ensure that you are eating live, fresh food at every single meal – foods such as raw salads and fresh, non-acidic fruit. A great way to supplement this is by juicing vegetables every day.

# Juicing

Non-acid fruits and vegetables provide the very best way for you to protect your health, and the quickest way to get large quantities of vital plant phyto-nutrients into the body is by making your own vegetable juice daily. Juicing large quantities of fruit and vegetables breaks the nutrient goodies out of their cellulose fibre casing, and turns them into a form that the body can easily digest. In this way, it is possible to get all the nutritious substances that your body craves without having to chew your way through many kilos of raw vegetables. The best juicer to buy is a press, because this does the least damage to those essential plant enzymes. Next best is the cheaper juice extractor, but purists say these machines do break up some of the powerful enzymes because they operate with a very high centrifugal force. Vegetables are very alkaline in nature, but many fruits are acid. So, make sure that your juices feature mainly vegetables such as carrots, beetroot, and celery, plus non-acid fruit like melons or papayas. Drinking a glass of vegetable juice a day can quickly restore the essential alkaline balance in your body.

## Recipes

Now, as my family and friends will no doubt testify, even though I have my moments, I don't purport to be a Gordon Ramsay in the kitchen. Accordingly, when I was forced to radically change my own eating habits, many of the foods that have since become a staple part of my diet were new to me. How to prepare some of them and how to combine them to make a tasty meal took a bit of time for me to get to grips with - and more than a bit of patience on my family's part too!

My advice is to invest a bit of time in getting to know your food, and a little bit of money in purchasing a few good recipe books. Personal favourites of mine include, 'The Healing Foods Cookbook' by Jane Sen and, 'Superjuice' by Michael van Straten.

## Stalkie's Workout

*Write down everything that you have consumed over the last two days. Note down in one column the live foods – the fruits, raw or lightly steamed/stir-fried vegetables, salads, nuts, seeds and raw cereals in your diet. When you have completed that, look at what percentage of live food you are eating. If you are eating 70% live food or more, then you are doing really well. If you are at 10% live, then that is a lot better than 0% and it is a starting point to improve your score.*

# Talking Toxins

Understanding what you should give your cells to keep them working properly is only half the story when you're learning how to lead a healthy lifestyle. You must also know how your body works with regard to toxins. You may feed yourself a lot of vegetables, but if you also consume a lot of toxins, then your cells will not be as effective. The main toxins we need to avoid in food are:

- Chemical additives put into food to extend its shelf life, or to enhance its colour and flavour. Some of these are even carcinogens themselves – look at the recent scare over the brown dye in a leading brand of sauce!
- Foods which are chargrilled or smoked, because these also contain carcinogenic substances.
- Alcohol and smoke - the two most common toxins which destroy our bodies' health.

Less well understood is the fact that the foods we need become toxic to the body if we over-eat them. This is because the body has to control the levels of all substances very finely in the blood – for example, sugar, protein, salt and fat levels are kept totally constant. But, if the body is regularly flooded with too much of these substances, it goes into collapse and the organs which control these levels become diseased.

This table shows the effect of eating too much of our basic foods:

|  | Excess Causes These Diseases | Key Organs Affected |
|---|---|---|
| Fat | Obesity, hardening of the arteries, heart attacks, strokes, cancer, arthritis | Heart and liver |
| Sugar | Obesity and diabetes | Pancreas and liver |
| Salt | High blood pressure, heart disease, strokes, obesity | Kidneys |
| Protein | High acid levels, cancer | Acidification of all tissues |

## Beware of The Effects of The Following!

### Fat

Excess animal fat from dairy products, meat and fried foods becomes deposited in the blood vessels and this, combined with high stress levels, is the reason why one in two people will die from heart disease. Some fat is necessary for the body to function efficiently; essential fatty acids from nuts and seeds, plus oily fish, are essential for health because they help to regulate cholesterol, maintain healthy skin and provide us with energy and insulation. However, most people eat far too much fat. Fatty foods are more readily available, and they're made to look very attractive when taking the form of ice cream, crisps and fast fried products. As a result, society has a real problem with obesity and this contributes to heart disease, breast cancer, and arthritis.

Many of these fast foods give you empty calories, with the result that you are overfed and undernourished. To keep fat levels down in the blood, the liver works very hard to lay down fat into the tissues; this exhausts us, putting stress on the heart and joints. Worse than that, the fat becomes a storehouse for chemicals from the environment, and also produces excess hormones, which fuel breast and prostate cancer.

## Sugar

Your body runs on sugar, after it has been broken down to glucose. All other foods can be broken down into sugar to keep you going, if your levels become low.

However sugar, like fat, is far more accessible in the modern diet than it was many years ago. Natural sugar called fructose used to come from ingesting fruits and vegetables, and this also provided many essential vitamins and minerals. Today, people tend to buy sweeter, processed foods including chocolates, biscuits and cakes, fizzy drinks, cocktails and ice creams. Sugar is also hidden away in the ingredients of products like baked beans, tomato ketchup and soups. High sugar intake has also been linked to serious health problems such as diabetes, heart disease and obesity. Put it this way: One Mars bar contains the sugar content of five pounds (2.5 kilos) of apples, and is absorbed into the bloodstream within 30 minutes. Just think how long it would take you to chew and absorb that level of sugar from all those apples!

## Salt

The body does need some salt to maintain the correct volume of circulating blood and tissue fluids. However, too much salt results in high blood pressure, which in turn can contribute towards strokes and heart disease. Most people consume far too much salt, and the main culprit is processed foods. This problem arises because the kidney gets stressed by excess salt; soon after, high blood pressure develops. This in turn puts you at risk of heart attacks and strokes.

## Protein

You do need protein to repair the wear and tear on your muscles, but you don't need it as a fuel food. Your body needs no more than 4oz or 120g of protein a day – so, it is easy to see that a day with bacon, sausage and eggs for breakfast, a cheese, chicken or tuna sandwich at lunchtime and fish, steak or chops for dinner will take you way over your protein requirement. Once you exceed your needs, the protein will be broken down and converted to fat for storage and producing acid in your body. Too much protein will also make you fat! Acid bodies lead to achy, rheumatic joints and also provide the ideal environment for cancer and arterial disease to develop.

## Tobacco

Mr Collins has never smoked; he's never really been interested, unlike his brother Ryan who has always been a smoker. Arthur does know that the effects of tobacco are dramatic. Smoking lowers the availability of oxygen to our tissues, and it raises blood pressure because carbon monoxide in the tobacco smoke reduces the blood's ability to carry oxygen. Smoking can cause many other problems apart from heart disease, including respiratory tract disorders and premature ageing of the skin.

The main problems are caused by carcinogenic tars in cigarettes, which cause cancer directly. But, smoke also causes fat to be laid down on our artery walls, increasing the risk of heart attacks; this can also cut off of the blood supply to our feet. Did you know that a significant number of smokers end up as amputees, because their limbs become too painful to bear when the blood supply is impaired? Smoking makes our skin look awful too, and we age quicker when we smoke because it destroys the elastin - yes, smokers wrinkle much faster!

## Alcohol

Nearly everyone is guilty of having a drink or two on most days, but in modern times we are also seeing a frightening epidemic of binge drinking, which is causing many young people to suffer liver failure by the age of thirty! The problem is, we see alcohol as being a socially acceptable drug, and people just don't recognise the risks. Alcohol is extremely toxic, and it effects every area of your body; not one of your cells is able to resist it. Alcohol causes dehydration, and this leads to hangovers. When alcohol breaks down, its products damage the liver directly, and as the liver struggles to metabolise away the poisons, many vital vitamins and minerals are used up, leaving the nervous system weak. So, those who drink a lot also become nervy and violent, with short tempers. Later on, they suffer from memory loss and sometimes, the nerves in their feet die too, meaning they can't feel the ground properly.

Remember that, for men, the safe daily limit is only one and a half pints of beer or three glasses of wine and for a woman, one pint of beer or two glasses of wine. It isn't okay to add up your whole weekly allowance and drink the lot on Friday and Saturday nights, because this type of binge drinking damages the liver even more quickly. Find other ways to feel good, relaxed and excited that don't involve poisoning your body!

## Caffeine

Caffeine, which most people consume in coffee, tea and fizzy drinks is a mildly addictive stimulant. When too much caffeine has been consumed, people can become over-anxious, restless and unable to concentrate. Some may also notice stomach pains, persistent headaches and sleeping problems. High doses of caffeine are toxic and can cause high blood pressure, heart palpitations and vomiting. All this occurs because the caffeine buzz puts us into fight or flight response, where our brain and muscles work at the expense of our digestion and immunity. So, they get more and more wound up, whilst we become less able to achieve any decent nourishment from our food - and, we get acid stomachs to boot.

## Working With Your Body

You are responsible for what you put into your body. Whatever goes into your body has to be digested, and then stored or purged in some way. When you become ill, your body immediately starts to try and cure it - this cure begins by eliminating toxins from the body. You eliminate toxins through urine and the bowel; you also get rid of toxins through the skin, the mouth and through the lungs.

The start of an illness can also be the start of the cure, provided you listen to, and work with, your body. If you think of a cat: as soon as they feel something is wrong they eat grass, and it makes them vomit. This is the beginning of the healing process, because they're getting rid of the toxins in their bodies. Humans are very similar; you have automatic responses for eliminating toxins, but you frequently mask these by taking drugs. The drugs get rid of symptoms like sneezing, coughing or diarrhoea, and yet these are the very things which are actually getting rid of the poison and starting the healing process.

So, don't just sit there being an accident waiting to happen. Be bright, be proactive and watch your energy and effectiveness zoom up as you start to work with, and not against, your brilliant body. The next chapter will help you to make the most of the knowledge you've gained so that you can TAKE ACTION!!

# The First Round
## *Getting Match Fit*

### 5 Raise Your Health Now!

### Taking Action

**Now, you should have a basic knowledge and understanding of how to treat your body - but it's using that knowledge that is important!**

Whether you wish to just improve your health, completely overhaul your fitness regime, or maybe overcome an illness, first you must construct a strategy, then you need to research how and when you are going to implement it. Finally, and most crucially, you need to instil the right attitude and determination to carry out your plan. In every case, your goal will be to radically improve your energy and wellbeing through:

**1** Increasing your oxygen levels
**2** Detoxing your body
**3** Improving your nutrition
**4** Drinking fresh water
**5** Taking regular exercise
**6** Relaxing your body and mind to energise yourself

Let's look at these actions individually:

# 1 Filling Your Body With Good Clean Oxygen

## *Stalkie's Workout (1)*

*Make sure that you are in a high oxygen environment, ideally outdoors or by an open window. Also, make sure that the air you are breathing in is clean and not polluted with smoke, chemicals or exhaust fumes.*

*Standing with your feet slightly apart, check that you are not holding tension in the chest wall, diaphragm or shoulders, by massaging or shaking loose any tensions. Relax the body and breathe out first. Then, practise taking a really good full breath that starts low down in the belly. When you do this it means that you are breathing from the diaphragm at the bottom of the lungs, so first let go of the stomach muscles and allow the belly to expand, then the mid part of the chest, going right on up to the tip of the lungs under the shoulders. As you do this, count in to six so that the in-breath is long, slow and smooth.*

*At the top of the breath hold it in for a count of three, and then equally smoothly breathe out again to a count of six, until the lungs are completely empty and the stomach muscles pulled in. Hold the breath out for a count of three and then repeat the process a further five times, until you have taken six completely full, deep breaths.*

*When you hold your breath at the top, oxygen in the air you have breathed in is moving into the blood stream. When you hold the breath out at the bottom, carbon dioxide is leaving the blood to go back into the lungs, ready to be breathed out again.*

*By practising this full breath you will achieve higher oxygen levels and lower carbon dioxide levels than you have experienced in a very long time! At first this may make you feel a little dizzy, because our bodies get used to working without the proper level of oxygen, and with far too much carbon dioxide in our system. So, start gently, and stop to rest if you feel dizzy. You will*

stir-fried or juiced

- Brown rice, brown spaghetti, couscous or quinoa
- Organic fish and occasional chicken or game
- Wholefood biscuits or cakes
- Wholefood snacks such as sultanas, dates, raisins, nuts
- Cereals, grains and pulses like muesli, porridge, lentils and red kidney beans

An ideal day could look like this:

## Breakfast
- Half a melon or a banana
- Bowl of porridge with maple syrup and oat milk
- An organic boiled egg
- Brown toast with honey

## Mid Morning
- Snack of banana, nuts and raisins and a vegetable juice

## Lunch
- Vegetable soup with brown bread, houmous and a fresh salad of grated carrots, beetroot, broccoli and bean sprouts with sunflower seeds and a good dressing

## Mid Afternoon
- Snack of wholefood cake or biscuit with a vegetable juice

## Supper
- Red chilli bean stew and brown rice with spicy stir-fried cauliflower OR
- Lentil shepherd's pie with steamed carrots and cabbage, followed by stewed apricots with maple syrup and soya ice cream

At this point, are you thinking there's no way you're giving up your breakfast of cappuccino, muffin and two Marlborough Lights? Or your mid-morning snack of a Danish pastry washed down with a cup of tea? Or your BLT sandwich at lunchtime, with a packet of crisps and a Coke? Or your supper of steak and kidney pie, potatoes, pre-packaged pizza and chips accompanied by a couple of glasses of Rioja? If you need a boost or a focus to change, then you ought to read 'Kate's case study' (in the 'Believe In Yourself' chapter of this book) and associate yourself with the pain of dying early from cancer or heart disease. Hopefully, this will give you the leverage you need for change. Here's a good tip for creating leverage - when you feel you cannot give up smoking or eating bad food, take the honourable step of apologising to your family, and say you are choosing food/alcohol/tobacco over life with them. This has jolted people into action before, making them at least try to give up their unhealthy lifestyles.

## 4 Drinking Fresh Water

Aim to drink three litres of good quality water per day. This means consuming 1 x 250ml glass or bottle of water per hour, which is not so much when you think about it.

The water you drink should be filtered or spring, as most tap water is very contaminated and full of chlorine! If you do not have a water filter, you could boil and cool your water as this gets rid of the chlorine, and precipitates out the heavy salts. You can then bottle and chill the boiled water, once it cools, in glass bottles.

This fresh water will wash away all the toxins that are being excreted from your body as you remove them from your diet and lifestyle.

# 5 Taking Regular Exercise

Build into your week:

- Two sessions of exercise in the fresh air. This could be walking, cycling, running or sports such as tennis, football, rugby, climbing etc. The aim here is to get your heart rate up to 100 - 120 beats per minute (from a resting pulse of 60 - 80). By raising your heart rate like this, blood is pumped around every cell of the body, working nourishing oxygen and nutrients deep into your tissues. This also prevents a build up of toxins and fatty deposits, and keeps the body really fresh and alive.

- Build a stretching routine into your day, so that your body becomes stretched and toned as well as fit. Learn some basic yoga stretches and twists by attending a yoga class, or buying a yoga video. This will keep you looking good, feeling great and will prevent your joints from seizing up prematurely. Yoga stretching also stimulates all the nerves and glands in your body, keeping you in tip-top shape.

- If you join a gym, make sure you are well supervised in order to get the right exercises for your body. Make absolutely sure that you relax and stretch before starting your gym routine, otherwise you will build the tension you're carrying into your muscular frame.

# 6 Relaxing Body and Mind to Energise Yourself

Another major factor to getting your body to work properly is learning how to let go. This will already be easier if you have stopped taking stimulants in tea and coffee, but most people who lead hectic, pressured lives with lots of goals and targets to hit, can become extremely tense and will need to learn how to switch off.

You may say "oh, I can relax easily, I just shut my eyes and I'm fast asleep," but, please realise that sleep is not the same as relaxation. If you go to sleep anxious, you have anxious dreams and will most probably wake up feeling just as tense in the morning. The best ways to get yourself truly relaxed are:

■ Buy yourself a really good quality massage from a complementary medicine centre. This will last for an hour, and if you tell the therapist that your focus is to get relaxed, they will use appropriate aromatherapy oils and massage strokes to ensure that you are deeply calmed. With due respect, beauticians are often taught to give quite superficial massages, and so the benefits may be only partial. If you go to a qualified massage therapist who's spent years in training, I can assure you that the results will be far deeper.

■ Another way to become very relaxed, and energised at the same time, is by having reiki, acupuncture, shiatsu (which is acupressure) or reflexology. These are all oriental therapies, and they are brilliant for releasing tension and re-energising the body.

■ Next, you need to learn how to relax deeply yourself, so that you can recognise and let go of tension wherever you are. Start this process by picking up a good relaxation tape from a complementary therapy centre, or health food shop. The beauty of this is, you can use it when you get home from work to calm yourself down, instead of reaching for a glass of wine or can of beer. When you learn to let go, all the energy you're burning in tension can be freed for your pleasure, and it will become more effective. As you calm down, you'll be able to think better, and you will find that you do less but achieve more.

■ Some people are so wound up and anxious that they need the services of a hypnotherapist before they let go. If you know that you are really anxious or panicky, get yourself an appointment to see a really good hypnotherapist or relaxation therapist who will talk you down into a much calmer state of mind. Try the following website for a list of good quality therapists, www.hypnotherapistregister.com

When you first become relaxed you may well go to sleep, because underneath your tension, you could be deeply exhausted. But, as you practise the relaxation response, it should become possible to calm down without falling asleep. The better you get at this, the more you will be able to recognise when you've taken on your tense body armour, and when you have your shoulders up around your ears! Then, once you are experienced at relaxation techniques, it's just a question of catching yourself and letting go. You will feel the sensation of relaxation and well-being flooding back into your system.

Just think about it all that energy that's going into tension could be used to make you feel great! The sooner you learn to relax and let go, the better you are going to feel.

Another thing that will improve greatly when you learn to relax is your sex life because, when we are tense, we can become numb and feel very little. It is therefore a really good idea to spend time getting yourself and your partner relaxed before sex, in order to really deepen the pleasure that you experience together. So, doing your relaxation tape with your partner when you get home from work can have far more benefits than just chilling you out!

Now, it is over to you - get thinking, get active and have some really good fun getting yourself strong, fit, healthy and brimming full of vital energy.

Raise
your
GAME
NOW!

# The Second Round
# *Gratitude and Attitude*

## 6 Gratitude and Attitude?

More often than not, Arthur Collins wakes up in the morning ready and raring to go to work, excited about the day ahead. However, until recently, when he came home in the evening, it would often be a different story. Mr Collins would not be happy; he moaned about how bad work was, and told his wife that her inability to have dinner ready on time had topped off the day! Mary Collins has always been a caring wife, and appreciates the fact her husband sometimes endures a hard day at work - but, she could not understand his strong reaction when the dinner was taking a long time to cook. As a result, Mary felt as though her husband did not appreciate her, nor the effort she put into each meal.

## Checking Out Your Attitude

In my experience, if people have a troublesome day, they tend to be in a bad mood as a result. Sometimes, work seems like a necessity - something you have to do. It can be tiring and fruitless, and as a result of that, you end up feeling down. The fact is, you can and do choose how things such as work affect you. From the time you wake up in the morning to bedtime, you choose how you act and react to things happening around you. Your choice of reaction to a certain situation can have far reaching effects on others.

When Mr Collins had a bad day at work, it not only influnced him, but also his wife. Although Mary may indeed understand when her husband's had a bad day, she could not previously understand why he had to take it out on her. The situation could always have been very different if Mr Collins remembered that, however bad a particular day had been, there would always be a loving family waiting for him when he returned home, and a tasty cooked meal as well. By choosing a positive reaction to the situation, Mr Collins could ensure that his family enjoy a nice meal together, without any bad feelings.

How you react to circumstances will have a direct bearing on the people around you, especially those who are closest to you - and these are the people that you really don't want to upset, because you care about them. When you take your bad mood out on family and friends, you often feel great regret and embarrassment later.

The attitude you adopt can have a ripple effect. Initially, Mr Collins' mood affected Mary, but it didn't end there; Mary spoke to her friend on the phone and moaned about her husband's lack of understanding, whereupon the friend went on to question her own partner's sensitivity - this led to her having an argument with him. He then went to his football game in a bad mood and played very badly, undermining the whole team's morale. All in all, Mr Collins' bad attitude had tremendous repercussions.

Your frame of mind has an effect on a large number of people including family, friends, co-workers, sports teams, the bus driver, the postman, customers, and suppliers - anybody with whom you come into contact. This exercise will show you how many people your attitude potentially affects:

## Stalkie's Workout

*Make a list of all the people that you come into contact with throughout your day. How many people have you listed? Now think about the number of*

Occasionally, Mr Collins went into work with a bad attitude. He talked to his colleagues in an unfriendly manner, and ordered them around. They in turn took on a similarly bad attitude when they spoke to the customers. On days such as this, Mr Collins' store did not sell as much as it should, and this put him in an even worse mood. The repercussions of Mr Collins' bad mood did not only affect other people - it affected the success of his business on those days as well.

This all sounds somewhat negative, but the same rule applies when your attitude is a positive one. The fact is, your attitude has an ongoing effect not only on the people you come into contact with, but also on your own potential success in life, and on your own well being. You need to manage your attitude for all these reasons, so making sure it's a positive one is extremely important.

## Being Grateful

Mr Collins works hard as a full-time manager in a retail shop for a large company; during his time with the firm, he's struggled to thrive in this role. Until recently, he's managed his store with a draconian attitude. Arthur used to believe that only his ideas and management skills could be the source of the store's success; it was either his way or the highway. Unfortunately, this type of management did not motivate his staff, and for this reason his store's success was limited.

Things changed when Mr Collins attended a motivational seminar as part of his company's Management Development Programme. He really enjoyed it, because people were relaxed, music was played, everyone had fun and he learnt a lot about himself and how people work. The seminar brought up many significant issues for Mr Collins which related to both his work and home life that he'd previously neglected.

The seminar made Arthur - as he now likes to be known - realise that gratitude is an essential component when adopting the right attitude. Arthur's now begun a new outlook on life, by really thinking about just how lucky he is; he's made a long list of all the things that he is grateful for. For example, he does not struggle with money, and he is in a secure job - consideration of these factors is making Arthur realise he should also be grateful for the gift of life. He did not work for it, he did not have to pay for it; life was given to him for nothing, and for this he is now thankful.

As a child you were cared for, fed and given clean water. Many people in the world are not so lucky. If you think about those who live in non-westernised countries, you are lucky, and wealthy beyond belief. With a roof over your head, clothes on your back and food on the table, you are among the top 10% richest people in the world (so we're told by the charities that work so hard to make life better for people of the Third World). I'm sure those people that live in a war torn environment just want to get on with their daily lives - make homes, enjoy and care for their families, and socialise with friends. In short, they would like to be free to enjoy the lives that have been gifted to them. It is rare that you think about these things every day, and you can be guilty of taking your good fortune for granted. If these things did cross your mind, more often than not it would affect you, whereupon you might choose your attitude with greater care. You would also realise how little reason there is to be grumpy, sad or impatient.

## Stalkie's Workout

*Sit down and think about all the things you are grateful for in your life. It could be that you have a great relationship with your family, it could be that you have the car you have always wanted, or it could be that you are grateful for life. Write a list of everything you are grateful for - try not to stop writing for at least 5 minutes.*

Following the seminar, Arthur has been able to open himself to a different way of thinking, and it has really been of benefit to him. He discovered that gratitude plays a vital role in adopting the right attitude. Now, when he faces a difficult situation, his first thought relates to something he can be grateful for, before he responds. If things aren't going well Arthur thinks about what he has got rather than what he hasn't, before starting to moan; in this way, he is learning to put the situation into perspective.

Arthur also learnt to ask himself the question "will I remember this problem in six weeks time, six months time or six years time?" The fact is, Arthur probably won't remember the majority of problems in six days, or even six hours time, therefore it really is not worth fretting over.

## Choosing Your Attitude

At the seminar, he learnt not only to be grateful, but also that he could choose his attitude; Arthur now knows only he has control of his feelings - nobody can tell him how to feel. Arthur's pondered this at length - he's never previously given much thought to his choice of mood, and how it affects both himself and others, before. Following the seminar, Arthur made a momentous decision; he chose to adopt a different attitude towards his life, and the events that happen in it.

The very day after making this decision, Arthur went into work, turned the music up full blast and greeted all of his colleagues with a hug before asking them: "who do you love, and what are you proud of?" The reaction to this, as you can imagine, was a mixture of shock, surprise, amazement and delight! In fact, the colleagues thought that maybe their boss had been on drugs! In reality, Arthur's behaviour now reflected his new attitude.

In recent times, the store has thrived. Sales have increased and morale is now high within the team. Arthur's store is currently one of the best performing in a company that has 500 of them - and the success is still growing. He's also found that his personal life has taken a positive turn. If he has a bad day at work - these are becoming rarer by the week - he doesn't take it out on Mary when he gets home.

Mary has recognised a lot of changes in Arthur; she asks lots of questions as to how and why he suddenly began to view everything so differently. The seminar sounds as if it was fascinating - now, she's started analysing her own behaviour. Mary, who always previously considered herself to be a positive person, realises that in some situations she is actually negative.

## Celebrating Life

Life includes some good experiences - birthdays, a new baby, passing an exam, getting a job, winning a competition are some of them. There are challenging ones too, including divorce, death of a family member and losing a job. Whatever the experience - positive or negative - you'll always view this in a very personal way.

Recently, Mary received the news that her best friend Jo's mum had passed away. Naturally, she reacted with sadness. Mary phoned her friend immediately to say how sorry she was for her loss, and asked when the funeral was. Jo was very sad too, but did not want her mother's funeral to be a sombre occasion where everyone wore black and cried. Her mother was a jolly lady, who always looked on the bright side. Jo wanted to celebrate her mother's life. Jo is also very grateful for the gift of life that her mother gave her, and wanted to celebrate that fact. She organised the funeral with upbeat musical accompaniment, and asked everyone to wear brightly coloured clothes instead of black; this Mary found strange.

After the funeral, Mary saw how happy her friend was and decided that a positive attitude towards life can produce a positive attitude in death. Mary thought this was a great example of how you can choose your attitude.

I think the majority of people feel as Mary did about a death in the family. Mary's personal view was that this represented a sad and sombre

## "You think **you've** got problems. You should see my piles."

occasion; that was her reality, and the label she attached to death. Jo put a new label on death - she celebrated the life that her mother had, and this is her reality. Mary had a negative attitude towards death, and Jo a positive one.

This is a rather extreme example of how Mary learnt that choosing an attitude can have amazing results; in this case, the lesson came from an upbeat funeral that people enjoyed. She also realised this experience echoed what her husband, Arthur, had learnt on his work seminar. You can choose your attitude to actions and events that occur in your every day life.

## Rethink, Reframe

Arthur and his brother Ryan have always enjoyed going to football matches, but even though they support the same team, they've very different views on what makes a good game. Arthur has a good time whatever the result; he simply loves spending time with his brother and enjoys watching live football. On the other hand, Ryan becomes very involved with the team and gets frustrated with the players when they do not perform well. Ryan becomes very angry after a poor performance by his team, and he usually abandons his brother, goes to the pub and gets drunk. The two brothers view football in a very different way.

Some people have a naturally positive attitude towards life, and others have a naturally negative one. In order to change from a negative attitude to a positive one, it is worth learning how to <u>reframe a situation</u>. To reframe a situation is to think about it in a different way - from an alternative perspective. If you want to change your pessimistic attitude to an optimistic one, you need to reframe a situation and see the positives in it.

Your answer to the common question 'is the glass half full or half empty?' indicates whether you are optimistic or pessimistic. A pessimist usually finds all the negatives in a situation, and an optimist all the positives. Regarding the death of Jo's mother, Jo focussed on all the positives in her mother's life: the fact she gave birth to her, her great relationship, and all the wonderful events her mother experienced. On the other hand, Mary focussed on the negative side - the loss. Jo's attitude was a positive one; Mary's was negative.

At football Arthur has a positive attitude towards the game whether his team wins or loses; he finds positives in any situation. Ryan, his brother, sees only the negatives.

What sort of attitude do you adopt? Complete the following quiz and all will be revealed!

## Stalkie's Workout

*Answer each question then add up the scores given at the end of each possible answer. Use your total score to find out about your attitude.*

**1 You have been pipped at the post for promotion. You think:**

   *a* It obviously wasn't the right time for me - my time will come. *(2)*

   *b* You can stick your job where the sun doesn't shine. *(1)*

   *c* What a brilliant learning experience. From now on I will always give 200% to ensure future success. *(3)*

**2 You were planning a day at the seaside but the forecast is stormy. You:**

   *a* Go anyway. You've got waterproofs, and it will be fun whatever the weather. The weather is in your heart. *(3)*

   *b* Change the venue and do something indoors instead. *(2)*

   *c* Sit and moan for the rest of the day blaming the weather for your misfortune. *(1)*

**3 An outfit you really wanted to buy is not in the shop when you finally saved enough money to get it. You:**

   *a* Curse the person who bought it and start crying. *(1)*

   *b* Think what a fantastic opportunity to look for something better that costs less. *(3)*

   *c* Go home and keep your money. *(2)*

**4 A crash on the motorway delays the traffic making you an hour late for a meeting. Do you:**

   *a* Be grateful that it wasn't you involved in the crash and make the most of an unexpected hour by telephoning some dear friends you need to catch up with. *(3)*

   *b* Sit and wait. *(2)*

   *c* Gradually get more angry and stressed until the point where this choice of negative attitude impinges on perfectly normal situations. *(1)*

**5** *You arrive at the airport to discover that you've missed the plane and the next one doesn't leave until the following morning. There is no other means of transport home. You:*

  *a* Enjoy the compensation and make the most of your evening in a four star hotel with free meal. *(2)*

  *b* Hurl abuse at the girl behind the desk until you're blue in the face. *(1)*

  *c* Use your initiative to try and swap tickets with other passengers in order to get yourself out on the evening flight. *(3)*

**6** *You're on a skiing holiday and there's no snow! You:*

  *a* Go walking and mountain biking in the alps, and enjoy the insurance pay out. *(3)*

  *b* Moan to every other holiday maker and make their holiday hell too. *(1)*

  *c* Sit in your room and pray to the snow gods. *(2)*

**7** *Your boiler breaks down in the middle of winter - you have no hot water and no central heating. You:*

  *a* Be grateful that you've still got a roof over your head and have fun camping out at home. *(3)*

  *b* Phone the boiler manufacturers and warn them that if they don't fix it immediately you'll not be responsible for your actions. *(1)*

  *c* Mope about, tell everybody you're cold and consistently repeat the story so that you live in a depressed state. *(2)*

**8** *Your partner is late for a date. You:*

  *a* Think he / she's stopped to assist an old lady that needed help. *(3)*

  *b* Think he / she's got involved in something at work, and has been unable to phone because the battery has run out. *(2)*

  *c* Swear they're having an affair. *(1)*

**9 You've been going to the gym for three months and not shifted a pound. Do you:**

  *a* Talk to the gym instructor to find out how you can get the result you require. (*3*)

  *b* Give up going to the gym immediately and eat three doughnuts. (*1*)

  *c* Struggle on without help. (*2*)

**10 You're going to start a diet. Do you:**

  *a* Think I'll start Monday and eat all the bad things you can to the end of the week. (*1*)

  *b* Start immediately - take a good healthy lunch to work. (*3*)

  *c* Go down the sandwich shop and order one round instead of two, but allow yourself extra mayonnaise. (*2*)

## Results

**Score 10 - 16**

You are very much like Ryan. When things don't go to plan, you get frustrated. You tend to look at the dark side, without considering the fact there could be a bright side. You don't intend to upset people, but you should be aware that your reactions are likely to affect and influence the people close to you.

**Score 17 - 23**

You are most like Mary Collins, in that you consider yourself a positive and fair person. However, sometimes you can be guilty of looking at the negative side of things. You don't do it on purpose, but there are occasions where things get to you.

**Score 24 - 30**

You are similar to Jo, because you always try to see the very best in every situation. Even when a tragedy occurs, you can be counted on to look at the positives, and your bright personality rubs off on others.

At this point, you should also be aware that your physiology can affect your

*attitude. Your non-verbal indicators; how you stand, how you hold your*
*shoulders and head, whether you walk quickly or slowly, with a purposeful*
*stride or a reluctant dawdle - all these can count towards a positive or*
*negative attitude.*

## Focus and Physiology

After attending the seminar, Arthur Collins realised that when he focused on the good things in his life, and events he was looking forward to (e.g. a night out with friends) he would always have a good day. His colleagues were soon able to guess when Arthur was planning a night out, and told him so. Arthur was amazed they'd spotted this, and asked them how they knew. His colleagues laughed, and said he would have a spring in his step that was unmistakeable. His better mood and natural body language gave the game away.

The thing to remember is this; your physiology can have a positive effect on you and your attitude, as can focussing on good things rather than bad. Focussing on the good will automatically make you stand and walk tall, put your chest out, breathe better, smile and generally look more positive. You will say more positive things (to yourself and to others), and feel better - just by paying attention to your focus.

But, even when you don't have anything positive to focus on, just changing your body language will have an amazing effect on the way you feel. Arthur's colleagues soon put this theory to the test in the shop. If they saw anyone with a bad attitude, they would get each other to stand up straight, stick their chests out and smile. This immediately changed how they felt, and had a direct effect on their attitude. The new feeling of positivity spread throughout the store - it was very infectious.

### Raise Your Game Now!

To demonstrate just how easy it is for your posture to affect how you feel, try these exercises:

**1** Put a pencil horizontally in your mouth, and try to frown. It's a very difficult task.
**2** Look down, slump your shoulders, breathe shallow and try to be happy. Impossible.
**3** Stand up straight, thrust your chest out, look up and put a big grin on your face. Try to feel depressed. You can't.

All three exercises show how your physical body can override your thoughts. Your brain is wired to receive messages, and your body is part of this. To have the right attitude, you must adopt the correct body language.

What you focus on can also have a powerful effect on your attitude, and you always have to focus on something - so, it might as well be something positive. Try this:

**4** Sit comfortably and don't focus on the colour blue. Don't think about anything blue - the sky, the sea, football strips, rivers and streams, your favourite sweater - nothing blue. Sit for five minutes. Okay, are you're five minutes up? Be completely honest with yourself. Did anything blue go through your mind? Of course it did. We have to focus on something, and the power of suggestion is very strong, as you have just discovered. Your focus will always make a difference, whether it is positive or negative, so focus on the good stuff.

## The Triangle of Communication

These three things can easily be remembered as the 'triangle of communication':

■ Focus - focus on the good stuff
■ Language - say the right things
■ Physiology - adopt positive body language, internally and externally

Your attitude can also be affected by your tone of voice, which we will be learning more about this later in the book.

## The Positive Effects of a Positive Attitude

In the New Oxford Dictionary, 'attitude' is defined thus: "settled behaviour, as indicating opinion." The use of the word 'opinion' in this definition makes you think that your attitude is a matter of choice. You form your own opinions, and you choose your attitude. Mary chose a negative attitude towards death, and Jo chose a positive attitude. You can choose to focus on the positive in your life, or the negatives. You can choose to adopt positive, open body language and send 'happy' signals to your brain, or you can do just the opposite. With all of this, you have a choice.

To illustrate the effect of choosing your attitude, try to imagine that you own an emotional bank account. The attitude that you take dictates whether deposits are made to this bank account, or withdrawn. A deposit will be made when a positive attitude is taken, or the positive reframing of a situation has been successful.

Let's imagine for a moment that it's raining, and the day's outing you arranged with the family has been ruined. You moan about living in England, say the weather is unpredictable, and complain that it's never possible to plan anything in advance. You describe the weather as being cold and grey; it makes you feel down and the only way through it, you decide, is to moan about it. This attitude and behaviour is an example of how you are making withdrawals from your emotional bank account. In adopting this attitude, you perceive a rainy day in the most pessimistic way possible. By doing this, you are handing over the control of your feelings and emotions to a completely unpredictable event - the weather!

Put a child in the same situation, and they won't moan or want to cancel a day out - it's just rain. It makes you wet, and then you get dry again.

In order to reframe this situation positively, you need to view it from a different perspective. This country does not suffer from drought; rain makes our grass green, and our crops grow. Plus, you can't jump in puddles without rain! In this way, you are investing in your emotional bank account. You are thinking of all the positives.

### Raise Your Game Now!

*There is scientific evidence to show that, if you adopt this positive view on life, the benefits are numerous and cumulative. You will be healthier; you will live longer. You will affect others in a positive way, and enjoy a lot more hours of happiness, fun and love rather than anger and frustration. The reverse is also true!*

Ryan does not run his emotional bank account very well. When he goes to watch his team play football on a Saturday, he expects a good performance so that he can come away saying he's had a good afternoon. When the team loses he shouts at the players, telling them they are useless, that they never make an effort, and that they always sit back and defend - he leaves them in no doubt that he's endured a bad afternoon because of it. Ryan never invests in his team; he does not encourage them when things are not going their way, and he just expects them to do well so that he can have an enjoyable afternoon. Ryan keeps making withdrawals, without any investment. His emotional bank account is definitely in the red, and he leads an unhappy life as a consequence.

When you invest in someone or something, it must be without expecting anything in return. When you invest wholeheartedly, it will come back to you - often tenfold. Do you only invest for a return? Would you only do a favour for a friend if they promise a favour back?

## Gratitude is the Springboard for Attitude

When you start your day with a few minutes of gratitude, it becomes the springboard for your attitude. Continue in the same way, and it is likely that your day will get better and better. This is true no matter what obstacles are put in your way, when you are grateful and choose your attitude. By keeping gratitude in your thoughts, you will make sure that every situation you encounter is processed in your mind in a positive way. This is the turning point.

Mary is especially grateful for life. She is not a religious lady; she finds it hard to direct her gratitude towards God, but it does go to the people she loves the most - her family. When Mary walks her kids to school in the morning, she has a small celebration. She celebrates her own life, and that of her children; this sets her up for the day.

You may find this strange to begin with, but as time passes it will become addictive - believe me, I know from experience! For a positive attitude to work effectively, action needs to be taken. Like the emotional bank account, if time is taken to make an investment, the interest and dividends will grow. If nothing is invested, there will be no return.

When you come into contact with people, think 'how can I make your day?' Try to think of ways you can make their day more pleasant and rewarding. It may be something very simple, like a quick chat or a 'thank you'. How about sending a card, letter or flowers, giving them a big hug or listening to them with sincere interest? Whatever it is, do it without any thought of repayment. Adopting an attitude of helping people spreads optimism and good feelings.

The more people you cheer up through your attitude, the more they will make your day in return, and the better you will feel. It's just like giving a present - it makes you feel happy and proud that you've made a difference to someone. Don't wait for a birthday or an anniversary to reward someone - just go out your way to give unconditionally.

If you are nice, you normally get nice behaviour back. The more you practise speaking positively to others, the more you will find it affecting you and your behaviour.

Remember that you will never get this day back; these minutes and hours are the only opportunities to live on this particular day - make the most of it. Of course, there will be times when there is tragedy and sorrow in life, and it will be hard to find a positive way of looking at the situation. However, there is still a choice. You influence the people around you all the time - friends, colleagues, family and children - by the attitude you take. Affect them positively or negatively; the choice is yours.

**For every 60 seconds of anger, frustration or hatred, you have lost forever a minute that could be filled with laughter, love or fun.**

"I have to do everything in this relationship...
this relationship...

all the exaggerating..."

# The Second Round
## *Gratitude and Attitude*
### 7 Take the Power Back

**Being able to choose your attitude, and reflecting it in your behaviour, has a powerful effect on your life and the people you mix with. Having discovered this, Arthur now enjoys a better work and home existence, while relationships in all areas of his life have improved. His business is more fruitful, and so is his marriage. Mary realises that positive thought can be very effective, even when she has to deal with the toughest problems. They have both discovered that gratitude is the key to the right attitude, which in turn goes some way towards creating a more fulfilling life.**

## Losing The Blame Mentality

At the seminar, Arthur also learnt that people who blame their predicament on others have what is called a blame mentality. People with blame mentalities never take responsibility for their own actions - Arthur realised that he was just such a person. When his store suffered a bad day of sales, he blamed the marketing department, the management, his colleagues, the location of the store, unrealistic targets - in fact, he blamed anything and everything except himself. It was then he realised he had to personally take the blame for much of what was going wrong with the store. He had to take responsibility, and take the power back into his own hands, rather than blame everybody else. It was at this point that Arthur decided to take a totally different approach to the management of his store - he chose the attitude that would allow him to support and care for his colleagues unconditionally.

As a result of Arthur's turnaround, Mary also took on board his new way of thinking. The two of them would discuss their friends and family into the early hours of the morning, finding wonderful examples of those who did and those who did not take responsibility for their lives and the events happening in them. Patsy, Arthur's sister, is a prime example of somebody who has a blame mentality.

Arthur's sister, Patsy, is married to Simon and together they have a son, Dan, who is six years of age. She gets on very well with Arthur's wife, Mary; they often have coffee together and talk about their respective families. Whenever the girls have chatted in the past, Patsy's usual topic of conversation centred around her workload being too much, and the fact she never had time to herself. As a result of this, Patsy found it difficult to talk to her husband, Simon, and give her little boy attention. Mary listened to Patsy talk about her problems like a good friend, but she couldn't help thinking that Patsy was just blaming her problems on everything and everyone around her.

Typically, Patsy would start her conversation on a high, before moving on to mention how much she was doing: shopping, ironing, DIY, caring for her child and so on. These are normal events that everybody has in their everyday lives - and yet to Patsy, they had become her sole focus, culminating in her constant feelings of being hard done by. A typical Patsy moan would be: "Simon should help out with the ironing, and Dan should tidy his room and do the daily chores. They take me for granted, and don't show me any love or appreciation! They expect it all to be done for nothing in return!" Patsy would then go on to justify how hard she worked, and how good she was; through the very act of doing this, Patsy actually believed her own words, but the reality was quite different. She really wanted more for herself than she was prepared to give to others, and became really quite scared of the truth.

Mary found herself sitting there thinking about Patsy's predicament. "You don't really want to genuinely help people - you don't want to support and love your family unconditionally. Your family probably know that whatever they do they'll get moaned at, so why bother even trying?" she thought. Mary wanted Patsy to discover what she had found herself - the ability to be really grateful for what she has, making for a more positive attitude towards life. Perhaps Patsy's existence would then take a turn for the better.

Sadly, Patsy had become a victim of her own choices; she did not take responsibility for her actions or reactions. She would take the easy route, blames others and justify to herself how hard done by she was.

## Are you a Patsy?

### Stalkie's Workout

*Answer each question and then add up the scores given at the end of each possible answer. Use your total score to find out whether you have a blame mentality.*

**1 You haven't managed to get everything done that you expected to achieve in the day. Do you:**
   *a Blame the phone calls you've had from others. (2)*
   *b Blame yourself for not being organised. (1)*
   *c Blame the person you live with for leaving the house in such a mess. (3)*

**2 You feel overwhelmed by your workload - do you:**
   *a Blame your boss/partner for expecting you to so do much. (2)*
   *b Blame your own delegation abilities. (1)*

*c* Blame your colleague/partner for not pulling their weight. *(3)*

**3 You have accrued rather a lot of debt on your credit cards. Do you:**
   *a* Blame your friend for taking you out shopping. *(2)*
   *b* Blame the salesman who made you buy something you don't need. *(3)*
   *c* Blame yourself for being such a sucker. *(1)*

**4 You get caught by a speed camera. Do you:**
   *a* Blame yourself for not keeping an eye on your speedometer. *(1)*
   *b* Blame the person you live with for being in the shower when you wanted it, making you late. *(3)*
   *c* Blame the government for putting a speed camera in an unlikely spot. *(2)*

**5 You have a minor accident, only to discover that you are not insured. Do you:**
   *a* Blame the insurance company for not letting you know that your insurance has expired. *(2)*
   *b* Blame yourself for not checking that it was up-to-date. *(1)*
   *c* Blame the other driver for stopping so promptly. *(3)*

**6 You don't like the holiday destination your partner has booked. Do you:**
   *a* Blame him/her for not discussing it with you. *(3)*
   *b* Blame yourself for not bringing the subject up sooner. *(2)*
   *c* Think going away somewhere is better than nothing. *(1)*

**7 Your luggage gets lost on a journey - do you:**
   *a* Blame the airline for not doing their job properly. *(2)*
   *b* Blame the check-in staff for labelling your luggage wrong. *(3)*
   *c* Think "oh well, there is nothing I can do" and get on with it. *(1)*

## Results

### Score 7 - 11

You are not a Patsy. But don't relax; it's easy to slip into the blame mentality. You are quite happy to be accountable for actions that you know are your responsibility. Keep up the good work.

### Score 12 - 16

Be careful, you are on your way to being a Patsy. You don't blame others all the time, but you tend to take the easy way out more often than not. Keep an eye on your attitude, and take responsibility.

### Score 17 - 21

You are a Patsy! You tend to blame others for things that go wrong in your life, even if they are unavoidable or your own fault. You think that you're not the problem - it's the others. Take a good look at your responses.

# Feeling Powerless

Patsy's old way of dealing with problems may seem the only way to go for many people, but in reality she was giving away her power and control. If you delegate someone the responsibility for making you happy, angry, sad or optimistic, then you have handed your power to that person. They are in control. Arthur handed over his control when he blamed the store's lack of success on his colleagues, the location of the shop and the weather; in reality, he was the manager and as such, Arthur should have taken responsibility.

The problem with Patsy was that she sincerely and genuinely believed it was the people around her who had the problem, and not her. Patsy got into the habit of blaming absolutely every situation she found herself in - every bad mood, every piece of bad luck and every depressing incident - on the people in her life.

Mary loves Patsy and wants to be a good friend to her, so she listened intently to all that Patsy had to say. Patsy also related how her parents still exhibited a bad attitude towards her; she said they always favour her brother and sister over her. She felt her parents treated her unfairly. Patsy even blamed her husband for what he did and did not do - she always complained that he never took her out, or bought her things.

This type of behaviour is self-destructive - at its root lay Patsy's very low self-esteem. She was incapable of taking responsibility for her actions, and chose instead to give her power away. The solution for Patsy? She needed to take the power back, just as Arthur did in his store. As an initial step towards this, Patsy needed to accept that she does in fact choose her own responses to situations. She needed to empower herself rather than others.

## Taking Control

Eventually, Mary conjured up enough confidence to face Patsy and challenge her about her incessant moaning. She spoke to her about taking control of her own actions. As a result, Patsy did try and take control, but she went about it in a negative way, and still didn't find the happiness she wanted. Patsy tried to take control over the other people in her life, but not her own actions.

One day at their usual coffee morning, Patsy told Mary that Simon, her husband, had booked them a table at a restaurant as a treat. Mary thought this was a nice gesture. Patsy, on the other hand, saw this as an opportunity to take control and see how much Simon really loved her. Patsy told Simon she was unable to make the date, and that she didn't particularly like the restaurant he'd chosen anyway. Patsy was hoping for a response such as, "don't worry darling - I'll find another restaurant that you like, and we'll go when it suits you." Simon actually replied, "no problem, we won't go then."

Patsy had always found it difficult to love others, mostly because she was unable to love herself. So, in order to make herself feel better, she needed

## "It's Mr. Wonder. He says he's just called to say he loves you."

to find a different kind of love. She craved attention, and resorted to a form of blackmail to get it. Simon was totally oblivious to Patsy's hidden agenda, and gave his reply "no problem, we won't go then" and thought no more of it.

# Losing Control

Simon's reaction to Patsy declining the dinner-date may have seemed perfectly reasonable to him, but it actually made her feel even more alienated and unloved because he'd not given in to her. Poor Simon was really in a no-win situation. Patsy was trying to feel loved by asserting control, but when things didn't go her way, she got upset by the situation and felt even less loved.

Patsy's aim was to try and receive more love; she wanted her husband to make her feel special. By saying that the date was no good, Patsy hoped that Simon would book another one at a different restaurant. From her viewpoint, if Simon did this he would be demonstrating how much he loved her, and that he would do anything for his wife, confirming that she was special to him and worth the changes.

Patsy didn't realise it, but she was behaving like a terrorist. She'd demanded more from Simon without even acknowledging the fact that he had done something positive by booking the dinner in the first place - Patsy had done nothing whatsoever. In fact, she told him she was fed up that he didn't choose the right restaurant, and that he didn't bother rearranging the evening. Instead of being grateful and viewing the dinner-date as a treat, Patsy looked at all the down sides to it. She also seemed to view it as a debt - as if Simon owed it to Patsy to take her out to dinner, even though she never takes him out.

Rather than loving herself for what she is, Patsy felt the need to test other people's love for her by pushing them as far as she could to see whether they would go that extra mile. But, pushing others like this is not the way forward. Patsy needed to take the power back and have peace of mind with who she is, rather than obtaining love from how others react to her. When she succeeded in changing the plans her husband made, Patsy was unable to find the proof of his love she so desired because it completely backfired on her.

Patsy was never in control of her own feelings - she put this control in the hands of others, including her husband Simon. When your feelings, such as confidence and self-respect, are only associated with the things that others think of (and do for) you, believe me, you'll never be truly happy. No matter how powerful you may think you are - no matter what personal qualities you possess - you cannot control what other people think or do. Mary recognised this in Patsy, and knew that she needed to empower herself rather than others. However, she also realised that taking the blame for your own behaviour is a bitter pill to swallow.

## An Exercise in Taking the Power Back

### Stalkie's Workout

*Write down five examples of the times you gave your power away, i.e. you blamed someone else for your current situation. Then, write down what you are going to replace those with. To help you, here are a couple of examples:*

**Ex 1:** *Judy used to blame her boyfriend for not feeling loved. Her new belief is that any time she wants to be loved, she should give love herself.*

**Ex 2:** *Alex used to believe that his current situation was the fault of his parents, because they favoured his brother and sister. His new beliefs are -*

- *my parents unconditionally love us all in an equal fashion.*
- *I love my brothers and sisters, and know deep down if any of us need support from our parents we shall receive it.*
- *my parents know that I have more to give, and were challenging me to make me stronger in later life.*

*OK, it's time for you to have a go yourself:*

**1 I used to blame**

................................................................................

**but now I believe**

................................................................................

**2 I used to blame**

................................................................................

**but now I believe**

................................................................................

**3 I used to blame**

................................................................................

**but now I believe**

................................................................................

**4 I used to blame**

................................................................................

**but now I believe**

................................................................................

**5 I used to blame**

................................................................................

**but now I believe**

................................................................................

## Taking Responsibility

Taking responsibility for our actions and responses is very hard to do, and many people are resistant to it. Some get angry when they realise that they don't choose their own responses to situations; maybe this is because such people think they have been fools, letting others control their feelings. Others simply think you just can't choose your responses. It is a very uncomfortable concept for these guys, because it's so much easier to blame others and think they are wrong, rather than look inside and think "I have been weak" or "I have been stupid letting others control me" and "I am really the one to blame." It is so much easier to blame other factors - the boss, spouse, parents, friends, work, weather or family - because personally, you are fine. The problem, then, is not with you; it is always with someone or something else.

Comments such as "the kids are really driving me crazy" or "my boss really winds me up" are typically heard when people are not taking responsibility for their actions. English people also tend to blame the weather for their mood. Mary knows full well what the weather is like in this country; she has been very understanding when listening to Patsy's whingeing, but even she found it hard to choose her response when her friend moaned in the winter about how the rain made her feel depressed. Then, when the summer came, Patsy said the heat was unbearable - and yet, she also claimed to be in a bad mood at work because she'd rather be at the beach enjoying it!

It is valuable to understand that it's not the weather which caused Mary to be in a bad mood - it was her response to the elements that made her feel down. You can choose your response; rain is going to happen, and it doesn't have that much of an effect. You can ignore it put up your umbrella and get on with life. Similarly, you can look for a new job if your boss really has a bad character. And, you can take the children somewhere interesting so they don't drive you mad. It is all about choosing a response that you are happy with - one that empowers you, and one that means you have taken responsibility, allowing you to regain control.

## Stimulus Response

If you get some pepper up your nose, you sneeze. The pepper is a stimulus; the sneezing is a response. Imagine that a friend jokingly pretends to poke you in the eye - you'll involuntarily blink, even though you know they're not really going to hurt you. These are examples of reflexes, which are automatic responses to stimuli, over which you have no conscious control. All humans are stimulus-response beings; however, there are responses that you can control, and which are not automatic. With these, you have a gap between the stimulus, i.e. what happens to you, and your response. In other words, between someone speaking harshly to you (the stimulus) and you getting angry (the response), there is a gap.

Having said that, where children are concerned, the gap between stimulus and response has not fully developed. Children respond instantly to stimulation by a comment, a situation or an action. Adults, on the other hand, do have this gap and can therefore choose how to respond. You can choose to allow your anger to develop, or to exercise patience. In every moment, this choice exists - there is always a choice.

These principles are very easy to understand, but quite challenging to put into practice. You are socially conditioned to respond in a certain way; hence, when the weather is grey and overcast, most people will moan. If a son or daughter behaves wrongly, they are conditioned to expect to be disciplined. A conditioned response to bad customer service in a restaurant is "let's not make a fuss - it will be alright". Taking the power back requires bravery and strength, and it demands us to be truthful with ourselves, which is often painful.

## Choose Freedom!

When you choose to take responsibility, you will feel liberated. By accepting that, no matter what your boss does or says he can never control how you feel, you'll no longer need to blame him or her for making you feel bad. How free would you feel if, whatever your wife or husband, boss or kids did or said, you could think to yourself: "I am choosing my response, and I am not going to hand over the power to them to control my feelings?"

Think: "I'm going to have a great day today, and I'm not going to let anyone else control it. I am in control of my life."

Mary persisted with Patsy, and tried to help her understand how acting like a terrorist would never get her the results she wanted. She told Patsy that she needed to take a long hard look at her own behaviour, and not that of other people. She explained to Patsy that the act of only making herself feel good when others do as she wants is a very negative way of travelling through life. In fact, Mary explained that, unless Patsy changed, she could lose Simon forever.

The penny finally dropped with Patsy - Mary was right. Patsy now realises that if she feels good about herself, it doesn't matter what others think; she can never control their thoughts anyway. She also now remembers what she has, rather than what she hasn't. Patsy now thinks, "this is the first time I have ever felt free. I did feel trapped - I put every effort into making people say nice things about me, and I wanted them to do as I wished. Realising that no-one can control my feelings, thoughts and emotions is liberating." Patsy has discovered a new sense of freedom and inner peace. Now, when anyone is ungrateful - or really grateful, for that matter - Patsy is equally as happy, because she's not letting anyone take 60 seconds of happiness away from her to turn it into a minute of frustration, anger or resentment.

Patsy changed her whole outlook on life when she started to take responsibility for her actions, and took her power back. Her conversations with Mary no longer revolved around her workload, and the lack of support she gets at home. This is primarily because she has taken responsibility, organised her time better and improved the levels of communication with her husband and son. Because Patsy is now more grateful for everything in her life, she also moans at her family less; as a consequence, they now support her more, and tell her how wonderful she is.

### *Raise Your Game Now!*

*When you take the power back, you will discover freedom. No one will be able to control you - only you will be in control of your own destiny.*

# The Second Round
## *Gratitude and Attitude*

### 8 The Real You

**What do you stand for? Have you ever considered writing a personal mission statement? If you were to die today, would your last thoughts and feelings be of contentment and satisfaction? Would you be happy with the way that you have conducted your life, with the things you have left behind? Consider all areas of your life, work, relationships, and children. Are you proud of all of your achievements in these areas? What would make you proud?**

## Values

Thinking about your life and what you stand for in this way will lead you to discover just what your values are. You may discover that you have values such as pride, loyalty, love of family and friendship. It is vital that you find out yours so that you know what your brain is focused on. When you know what your values are then you are more self aware – you will know what is important to you, what you want to avoid and so on. This knowledge can be a new beginning for you. If you can determine your values, change them for the better and act upon them, you will be sculpting a fulfilling life for youself.

Arthur was asked to think about these things in the seminar he attended and was initially stumped by the questions. He knew he valued his friends and his family, he loved going to football with his brother, he loved having a few beers with his mates on a Friday but he was fairly confused about values. In his heart he says he knows what he likes - friends, family, good times; he knows he is a caring, loving person and he wants to make the most of his life. What followed was very powerful and moving for Arthur. It was an exercise that really challenged his ideas.

## Your Values And <u>What</u> You Value Are Different!

This exercise involved Arthur imagining he'd been kidnapped. He had to come up with words that he would want his friends, family and colleagues to use when describing him to a journalist who was writing about him. The answers would show how he would like to be remembered.

He wanted his family to say he was caring, supportive, loving, loyal, always there, exciting, a good laugh, passionate and trustworthy.

He wanted his friends to say he was trustworthy, honest, comforting, fun, inspiring, a good laugh and the life and soul of the party.

He wanted his work colleagues to say he was hardworking, supportive, positive, loyal, a natural leader, good decision maker and if a sensitive subject cropped up he was courageous in his approach.

He wanted his team members to say he was supportive, cheerful, optimistic, always wanted to win, turned up on time and was a good listener - and he never forgot the oranges at half time!

The list of words and phrases produced in this exercise amount to Arthur's desired values. This is how he would like to be seen. His list was:

Caring, supportive, loving, loyal, always there, exciting, a good laugh, passionate and trustworthy, honest, comforting, fun, inspiring, a good lover, the life and soul of the party, hardworking, positive, a natural leader, good decision maker, courageous, cheerful, optimistic, always wants to win, he turned up on time and was a good listener. Now you can try this exercise for yourself and discover your own desired values:

## Stalkie's Workout

*Imagine you have been kidnapped in a foreign country and it is very likely that you will be killed. Back home a journalist is writing an article about you for a national newspaper and asks a close friend, a family member, a work colleague and a person from your football team/choir/club/church to describe you. What would you like them to say? Choose five words you would like them to use.*

**Close friend**

**Family member**

**Work colleague**

**Team member**

What you have just written are the emotions and behaviours that you personally value. Your values are represented here by how you would like to be seen by others. Once you have finished, read your values over and ask yourself this question:

## Are Your Actions Moving You Towards Your Values?

Now consider whether everything that you have just written is true. If your friends had to tell the truth, is this what they would say about you? Would there be any changes to the words you have chosen?

Often your behaviour does not reflect the way in which you would like to be remembered. This exercise is helpful to enable you to assess your values, and also to see how they are reflected in your behaviour.

Arthur did this exercise alongside his colleagues at the seminar. But they did something in addition to this. Arthur's colleagues were also asked to come up with words that described Arthur's behaviour. They were as follows:

- Strict
- Patronising
- Harsh
- Hardworking
- Focused

Now, Arthur felt really quite good when completing this exercise and felt very buoyant about what a great guy he was. Until you hear what people describe you as, the penny doesn't drop. Many go through life thinking how wonderful they are (and, in effect, how they would like to be remembered if they were kidnapped), but the real acid test is to get someone to tell you honestly how it is.

Most people would not like to be told by others how they really are, and most others are too embarrassed to give people true feedback that can be acted upon. What usually ends up happening in most people's reality is we don't learn the truth. Therefore, we lose sight of our values and how to achieve them through the correct behaviour.

Here, Arthur has not only thought about how he would like to be remembered, he has also got some honest feedback so that he knows how it really is. With this in place, Arthur can now write down or discuss with his friends, co-workers and family the behaviour he needs to carry out in order to be the loving, caring, passionate person he desires to be.

Let's delve further into Arthur's exercise and see what else can be learnt from it:

Arthur highlighted his wish to be hardworking, supportive, positive, loyal, a natural leader, a good decision maker and, if a sensitive subject needs to be approached, courageous.

His colleagues said that he was strict, patronising, harsh, hardworking and focused.

Arthur asked his colleagues why they thought as they did. What makes him harsh, for example? They replied that he doesn't let them finish making a point, he only focuses on the bad and forgets the good bits they have done. If they do something wrong he is on them like a ton of bricks, whereas they can do ten things right and he will say nothing. Arthur's desired values were 'supportive' and 'positive' but his colleagues described him as the opposite!

The outcome for Arthur and his co-workers here was to agree upon a set of behaviours. For example, when a colleague did a number of things right, Arthur's new positive behaviour would be to acknowledge that and congratulate them. When a colleague did something wrong, Arthur would; 1) not let it fester, 2) always remind them of the good points and, 3) separate the behaviour from the person. This meant that if he pointed out something they did incorrectly he would reprimand the behaviour but reassure the person. Where Arthur's behaviour was unduly harsh, such as never letting his colleagues finish a sentence, his new behaviour would be to seek to understand, before being understood.

Such discussions enabled the whole values 'thing' to become quite clear to Arthur. Although he genuinely did value supporting people, he hadn't previously behaved like it. After this exercise, Arthur can genuinely live in line with his values. He now knows the behaviour to adopt when it comes to supporting his colleagues. When he thought about this and was honest with himself, he realised he was like this, not just at work but outside of it too - he may have valued being a supportive husband but he didn't often act like it; he often mentioned the bad things to his wife but more often forgot the good.

> *Raise Your Game Now!*
> *Living in line with your values means that you back them up with your behaviour. If you love, care and support - the love, care and support you get back will prosper. Give and you will receive.*

Creating an environment where your values can be appreciated by others and vice versa, gives a real opportunity for honesty, love and personal growth to thrive in all your relationships - whether at home, socially or at work. It is tremendous to live life this way.

## Moving Closer To Your Values

In order to move closer to your values and reinforce them with your behaviour, it is useful to write down a few thought provoking questions. Look back at the words you used to describe how you would like to be remembered, then put together some questions based on these values and emotions. For example:

■ Who do I love and when did I last tell them?

- Who loves me and when did I tell them how much I appreciated their love?
- What am I grateful for, and who have I let know?
- Who am I proud of, and when did I last tell them?
- What am I excited about and when did I share it?
- Who do I trust and when was the last time I let them know?
- Who do I respect and when was my last action to demonstrate this?

## Being True To Yourself

What happens if you do not live in a way that is true to your values? After Arthur had attended his motivational seminar he encouraged his brother Ryan to complete the exercise to discover his values. As Ryan began to do the exercise, he realised that he had never thought about himself and his values in this way before. He had chosen his route in life and it was one that took the smallest amount of energy. He had a negative attitude; he never used to give to others and he was always the one to take. As a result of this behaviour he was very unhappy – as were his family and his colleagues - but he had no idea why. The more this continued, the more immune Ryan became to people's feelings. He didn't really think about emotions at all, and saw little point in caring for others unconditionally because he couldn't see what good it would do him! The exercise brought a few things home to Ryan and he started to change his views and his behaviour.

> ### Raise Your Game Now!
> *Caring for others is a natural principle – a principle being an external force. For example, if you forget to water a plant, wherever you live in the world it will die. If you do not care for your customers, friends or loved ones they will leave you – whatever kind of business or lifestyle you have. These are natural principles.*

There is a great power to be found in caring for others and giving unconditionally. If you do something for another person without pay or even the expectation of a reward, your life will be richer and more fulfilled.

## Our Three Separate Lives

Arthur learnt a lot from the seminar and his quality of life has improved greatly at home and at work. One of the things that really impacted upon him was the realisation that he actually lives <u>three separate lives</u> – one of which makes you realise just how vital it is to live to the values you stand for.

The three separate lives that apply to all of us are:

- **The external you** – this is what everyone sees in public. It can be in a public place such as a shopping complex or it can be at work dealing with customers, suppliers or colleagues. It is wherever you are seen out and about, living your life.
- **The internal you** – seen by your very close friends, family and loved ones, this is the intimate side of you. Whether it is a good side or a bad side, it is the side you will only demonstrate or show when you feel very close and secure and in a very private situation.
- **The hidden you** –this is where you are thinking what you stand for - when you put your head on your pillow and you consider how you acted during that day. Only you will know whether you have acted with courage, with integrity and love. This is not about what your co-workers or even your loved ones think about you, this is only whether <u>you</u> are comfortable with you.

By carefully considering the importance of this third 'you' – the hidden you - you will realise just how vital it is that you find ways to live in harmony with your values. If you are living according to the values that matter to you, then you will feel contented when you're alone with your thoughts. If however, there is an emotion that you value such as honesty, and you have persuaded everybody how honest you are but you really know you have been dishonest, then most people would be eaten away by this and feel very uncomfortable. In many cases this can lead people to feel eternally unhappy, because they are not living a true life. Whatever the emotion is that you value (honesty, courage, true love…) but live without, the real you will hurt.

## The Undesirables

Now we need to identify the flipside to your values. This time we're looking at those behaviours that are <u>undesirable</u> to you. These are the opposite of the values we examined earlier - your 'anti-values', your behaviour to avoid.

Some people find this task quite hard to do well. Just ask yourself what you would like to avoid and what emotions or feelings you really hate. Is it embarrassment, anger, hatred, a feeling of being overwhelmed or out of control? It could be loneliness, boredom or disappointment. To help you with this, do the following exercise:

### Stalkie's Workout

*Imagine you are creating your perfect day. Examine an average day for you, thinking about all the things that happen and the people you meet, then take out of it all those emotions that irritate or upset you. Remember you're trying to create a day in your life when nothing at all happens to mar your enjoyment. You will need to consider all the different areas of your life to make sure that you capture all those negative emotions that get in the way of perfection.*

*Now write down your answers to these questions:*

**1 What's most important for me to avoid at home?**

........................................................................................

........................................................................................

**2 What's most important for me to avoid at work?**

........................................................................................

........................................................................................

**3 What's most important for me to avoid in my family?**

........................................................................................

........................................................................................

**4 What's most important for me to avoid in my friendships?**

........................................................................................

........................................................................................

**5 What's most important for me to avoid in my relationship?**

........................................................................................

........................................................................................

When Arthur did this exercise, examining the five areas of his life, he found the 'anit-values' that he did not want in his life – in his perfect day – were as follows:

- Dishonesty
- Unscrupulousness
- Petty mindedness
- Narrow mindedness
- Misery
- Miserliness
- Selfishness
- Bigotry

# The Affect of Values

If you've carried out these last two workouts carefully, you, like Arthur, will now have lists of two distinct sets of values – one list of your desired values and another of your undesired ones. Having opened his eyes to how his values could affect his life, Arthur moved on to looking at how he needed to live his life in line with his desired values whilst avoiding the undesirables.

This is what he came up with:

**The actions I am going to take immediately are:**

- I am going to be more supportive of Mary – I am going home tonight and will ask if there is anything I can do around the house instead of just watching the TV.
- I am going to spend more time with the children and try to have more fun with them, starting by playing the game with James that he wanted to play the other day but I didn't have the time to do. I'm also going to tell them how proud I am of them.
- I am going to listen more at work and be less dictatorial. My colleagues sometimes know better than me. I am going to have meetings with individual colleagues tomorrow and ask them what they want to achieve and how I can support them.
- I am going to have more fun with my friend John – I am going on the Internet tonight and booking tickets to see a band.
- I am going to help Ryan to stop smoking, support him and get him interested in doing something healthier – like playing badminton with me once a week.

Now you too can do this exercise and find areas of your life where changes in your behaviours will mean that you bring your life into line with your desired values.

## Stalkie's Workout

List the 5 biggest areas you need to address in order to move closer to your positive values and avoid the negative values.

(If you are living in exact accordance with how you would like to be portrayed – where there is no room for improvement – ask yourself how you can take your life to the next level and what behaviour can help you to do that.)

1 ........................................................................

........................................................................

........................................................................

2 ........................................................................

........................................................................

........................................................................

3 ........................................................................

........................................................................

........................................................................

4 ........................................................................

........................................................................

........................................................................

5 ........................................................................

........................................................................

........................................................................

By recognising these areas, you are now in a position to do something about them...

## Stalkie's Workout

Write down 5 actions that you are going to complete today to move you closer to one of your values. If you would like to be remembered as loving and you believe that you need to improve in this area, then an action could be to ring your friends and family and tell them that you love them.

Write 5 action points that you are going to do now:

1

2

3

4

5

Now, take this further. Commit to taking action within the next month:

Write down 5 actions you are going to carry out within the next four weeks:

1

2

3

4

5

Remember, you must take action in order to make any changes. Now you are sure of your values, you will be able to find out why it is that you feel a certain way about events, relationships and situations in your life.

# The Second Round
# *Gratitude and Attitude*

## 9 Believe In Yourself

**As a result of taking the power back, Patsy has begun to believe in herself and her abilities - her life is going from strength to strength, and she is now a stronger and better person. Simon responds to Patsy in a more positive way, and her son Dan loves to be with her.**

Meanwhile in his store, Arthur has become more successful, because he too has started to believe in himself and his abilities. Both his personal confidence and the store's prosperity are on a self-perpetuating upward curve. The more he believes in what he is doing, the more successful Arthur becomes; as this level of successes grows, his self-belief takes a further boost, and so the cycle goes on. Without doubt, this is an incredible time for Arthur.

*Belief is the mind's powerhouse. Gratitude, the right attitude and taking the power back all lead to having greater self-belief.*

Belief - it affects who you are, how you think about yourself and how you live your life. However, beginning the journey to a sincere belief in your abilities is a very challenging process. In order to help you on this journey, you need to understand what belief is, how positive and negative thoughts affect your life and how you can control your confidence.

# What Is Belief?

In the Concise Oxford Dictionary, belief is said to be; "acceptance as true or existing (of any fact, statement etc)". In 'Awaken the Giant Within', Anthony Robbins defines belief as a 'feeling of certainty'. You can also consider belief to be a feeling about an event or situation that is based on past experiences and desires. In short, your belief is influenced in four different ways:

## Environment

Patsy used to believe that the state of her life was down to everyone else. She was brought up by unsuccessful parents, who also had 'blame mentalities'. In turn, they blamed their life problems on their parents, their education, the amount of money the family had and so on. It was the environment that Patsy was brought up in which influenced her own belief that everyone else was to blame.

## Events that occur in life

Before Arthur became the manager of his own store, he worked for an accountancy firm. The firm was run in a very traditional manner; you never questioned a partner, and you only spoke when you were spoken to. This way of working was instilled in Arthur, hence the way in which he ran his shop. These past events in his life led Arthur to believe this was the only way to run a business.

## Knowledge

Knowledge also affected Arthur's belief in how he should manage a store. Arthur only ever knew the formal way in which the partners treated him at the accounting firm; his knowledge was a direct result of this experience. Patsy was also unaware that there could be another way of managing her day - a way that made her more time-efficient, more capable, and more available for her husband and son.

## Results

When Arthur was learning from the accountants, he saw and experienced the results that would be achieved if you did and said things in a certain way. He remembered these from being in a formal environment and, gaining knowledge and seeing results, he therefore chose to use the same principles in his shop. It wasn't until he learnt some alternative management methods that his belief was shattered and a new one formed.

## Our Different Beliefs

Kate, the eldest daughter in the Collins family, is at an awkward age; she has encountered problems because she believed that she is unattractive and overweight. Kate believes that if she lost some weight, she would be a lot happier. If she was slimmer, Kate felt, this would lead to greater levels of acceptance by her school friends too. In truth, Kate desperately wanted to feel proud of her body, so that she could be confident the boys would find her attractive, while the girls would want to like her. Kate has never been a slim girl, and her weight had always bothered her a little - but now, hitting the teenage years, Kate's weight was becoming a really big problem.

Mary had always thought her daughter fine just the way she is, although Kate's recent interest in her weight had prompted Mary to consider what would be best for her child's health. She could see that Kate believed her weight was holding her back from being in the right crowd at school, i.e. from being accepted by the popular girls and wanted by the boys. Mary became afraid that, should Kate's weight continue to rise, it might have damaged her health. Both Kate and her mother were convinced that what they believed about the situation - Kate's weight - was true. However, their respective beliefs had come about through totally different sets of life experiences.

Kate and Mary had different beliefs because of the four main influences: environment, events, knowledge and results. Mary grew up in an environment where health was always considered to be the most important thing; she has, therefore, always been very cautious when it comes to her children's wellbeing. Her belief that Kate's weight was a health issue, rather than a popularity one, was based on this. Mary also believed that the images fed to her daughter via television and magazines were unrealistic, promoting as they do the wrong idea of why someone should lose weight. Mary knew that teenage girls do fluctuate in weight, but this knowledge also led her to believe that it is something to keep an eye on from a health point of view. By looking after her children's health, Mary's mother made sure they never missed a school day; the results of this are clear to Mary, and the experience adds to her beliefs.

On the other hand, Kate had a completely different set of beliefs. Her thoughts on how teenage girls should look were based on the pictures in magazines, and she had grown up in an environment where the stick thin girl was the popular girl. She believed, therefore, that she too should lose weight in order to be a member of the 'in crowd'. Kate could see that her school friends were far more interested in talking to the 'cool' girls, who were slimmer than she was. Her belief was that, if you are slim, then you will be popular. Kate had only ever known this way of looking at the situation, and believed she urgently needed to lose some weight, otherwise she would never get to where she wanted to be. The results of being slim and attractive were seemingly obvious to Kate.

## Stalkie's Workout

*How do you see yourself?*

*To understand the difference between how you see yourself and how your friends and family perceive you, write down ten words that you think accurately portray yourself. Next, ask between three and ten others to come up with ten words that describe you. Now, compare the lists - see how similar or how different they are. The more similar the words, the more you are behaving as you believe, with the opposite being true if you find yourself counting up quite a few differences.*

# Self-Belief

Self-belief is a set of ideas we have about ourselves that we consider to be true. These sets of ideas become our self-image. Kate's self-belief was that she had become overweight and unattractive, and therefore she'd never get to where she wanted to be. She believed she needed to be slim in order to fix the situation.

## *Stalkie's Workout*

*Uncover your self-beliefs:*

   *Try and establish what beliefs you have about yourself with the following exercise. In order to understand how self-belief is built up, consider how you came to believe the ideas that you have about yourself.*

   *Write down 10 beliefs that you have about yourself - for example, "I am a very loyal friend, I am a hard worker, I love life" and so on. Then think about why you believe these things, and write down those reasons too.*

**Kate did this exercise, the highlights of which were:**

- I believe I am fat because when I compare myself with models featured in magazines and on the television, I am bigger.
- I believe I am unattractive because I don't look like the women in the magazines - no one would want to take a picture of me.
- I believe I can't attract boys because they always want to go with slim, attractive girls.
- I believe I can't be a part of the in-crowd because they only mix with

slim people.

Kate found this a very difficult and upsetting exercise to do, because she could not think of many positive beliefs she had about herself.

**Mary did the same exercise about Kate, and came up with the following;**

- I believe that Kate is a very beautiful girl who doesn't need to look like the models featured in magazines, because they are not true, real-life images.
- I believe that Kate should only worry about her weight with her health in mind.
- I believe Kate should be content with her weight, and that she must not do anything to harm herself just to lose a few pounds.
- I believe Kate is extremely attractive because she is funny, talented and loyal.

The two women's beliefs were completely different, based on their differing environments, past events unique to them, their knowledge, and the results each had achieved.

Kate believed that her weight was responsible for making her feel negative about herself. Beneath the surface, however, it was her desire to be accepted by all the right people - that had become Kate's driving force. She wanted to be proud of herself, and to have confidence. If she could achieve the acceptance she desired with the 'cool' crowd, how would this make her feel?

Kate could have quite easily become fixated about her weight, potentially leading to health problems. She found herself in a raw emotional state as it was, because she thought she was unattractive, leading to feelings of being unloved, insignificant and insecure. In this state, Kate could have chosen to get her needs met in a negative fashion; she might have started to self-harm in order to achieve love, to feel she had done something significant, and to be secure in the knowledge that she had people about her who would come to her aid, for example.

# Developing a Positive Self-Belief - Kate's Case Study

In order for Kate to develop a positive self-belief, she needed to embrace the following points: be grateful for what she has, have the right attitude, and take the power back. She also needed to ask herself the right questions, and use the right language; create leverage for change; use a technique called 'visualisation'; take action; celebrate each step along the way; use her natural tool kit - the Reticular Activating System.

# The Reticular Activating System

The Reticular Activating System - RAS for short - is a group of cells in the base of your brain stem known as the 'control centre'. The RAS is primarily responsible for arousal and sleep; it controls your getting up in the morning, and your ability to sleep at night. Your little control centre also sorts and evaluates all incoming data. The Reticular Activating System is responsible for filtering out the urgent stuff from the unimportant, so that you are able to function properly and effectively.

Your RAS is part of your natural tool kit; it helps you to see the information that you need to. Have you ever noticed, for example, that once you've decide what type of car you would like to buy, you can't stop spotting them going down the road! This is your RAS at work. It causes you to find and notice things that are associated with what you have been focusing upon. Therefore, whether your beliefs about yourself are positive or negative, your RAS will still work in the same way, i.e. by finding the things that you are focusing on. In other words, your RAS will always find justification for those beliefs because your mind wants to prove you right, not wrong.

So, because Kate only believed the negatives about herself, she could only find evidence apparently confirming these were true. She would only ever see slim people in magazines and on television; she would only notice boys who asked out the slim girls. In other words, Kate was only able to notice the events around her that "proved" these negative beliefs were right - to Kate's mind, slim was attractive.

On the other hand, if she could believe positive things about herself, then her RAS would validate these as true instead. As we know, Kate wanted to lose weight in order to make herself feel better; after taking this decision, she had started to find lots of magazine articles and books about dieting. She'd noticed how many healthy alternatives there were for snacks in the local shop as well - Kate had never really seen these things before, because she'd not been focusing on losing weight. This was Kate's RAS at work.

As well as drawing your attention to the things you are focused on, the Reticular Activating System filters things that are unimportant, or that you don't want to concentrate on. For example, the noise of trains going by may annoy those who move into a house near a railway line; after a short time, however, the RAS will activate and they will no longer be bothered - because they won't even notice it anymore.

### Raise Your Game Now!

*The Reticular Activating System is the key to turning on your brain. It is a very complex collection of neurons, and these form the point of contact between signals from the outside environment and your own internal world. In other words, it is the part of the brain where the world around you and your inner thoughts and feelings meet.*

# Gratitude, Attitude and Taking the Power Back

For Kate to feel good about herself, she first needed to become aware of how lucky she is. She should be grateful for what she does have, rather than focusing on the negative, i.e. her belief that she is overweight. Once she had found gratitude, Kate could begin to feel good about herself, thereby opening the way for her to instill the right attitude.

Once she had gratitude and the right attitude towards her predicament, Kate could make the progression towards her goal. The next step would involve taking responsibility for the way she was; nobody else could control her thoughts and actions - including what she put into her body - and only she would suffer as a result of what she was doing.

## Thoughts and Actions

The power of your life evolves from the quality of the internal thoughts you have, and your ability to take action upon them.

A thought is an internal question; when you think about something, you are asking yourself a set of questions.

Whenever Kate went to a restaurant and looked at the menu, she would inevitably ask herself questions such as "shall I have a starter? What do I fancy - the fish or the lamb? What is the healthiest thing on the menu? Should I order dessert?" Whatever her answers to these questions, Kate's train of thought would continue, for example: "If I order the salad, should I leave some and state that I am full to show I'm not greedy?" Whatever Kate's questions happened to be on a particular day, they were always internal - rather than asking out loud whether she should finish her meal to avoid looking greedy, she would just eat the meal, give herself the answer internally and act accordingly.

It's important that these internal conversations are stated positively. If you ask yourself a negative question, then you will get a negative answer.

If you have a meal in a restaurant and ask yourself whether you should stop eating because you're afraid everyone will think of you as a glutton, the enquiry is made with a negative presupposition. If you think negative thoughts, you will end up justifying them to yourself. You will believe others are looking at you and thinking you're exactly what you suggested to yourself. In actual fact, they are probably not paying any attention to you at all - but, your brain will justify your negative thoughts because it does not want to make you out to be a liar. Your RAS will be working to help prove you are right.

To get answers that will transform your life, you must ask the right questions. So, whether you think you can or can't, you are probably right! If Kate, therefore, could tell herself that she can lose some weight, and stated her goals along the way in the affirmative, then she will achieve.

There are so many examples in everyday life where people tell themselves that they can't do things. They believe they can't lose weight because of their genes; they think they cannot give up smoking because it's an addiction - and no one can beat an addiction. This is self-justification, and it can occur when people don't have a big enough reason to make the change, they don't want it enough, or they haven't got the courage.

By saying these things, people can back themselves into a contrary corner. What these people are doing is disempowering themselves by giving their will away to the cigarettes or their genes. Kate needed to empower herself.

## Leverage for Change

In order to change her negative self-belief, Kate had to first understand that all actions in her life are designed to either avoid pain or gain pleasure. As things stood, Kate was in a position of pain; she did not feel good about herself and wanted to be in a better place - a pleasurable place. In order to change this, she first needed to create some leverage.

# Personal Transformation System (PTS)

A burglar uses his crowbar to open a locked window - this is his leverage. Similarly, Kate needed to find something which could act as a leverage while attempting to change her behaviour of eating too much of the wrong kinds of food. In order to do this, Kate would need to associate pain with the wrong kind of food, and pleasure with good food and exercise. This is how she went about it in seven steps:

## Step 1 - Creating Negative Leverage

Kate needed to ask herself the following questions in order to gain negative leverage, i.e. to make herself feel really bad:

### What pains are my current beliefs causing me?

I believe I am fat, unattractive and unpopular. I eat because it makes me feel better and helps me forget who I am. After I've eaten I feel even worse because I know I have not helped the situation.

### How will I feel in five years time?

I won't have the confidence to go on holiday in hot countries and show my body; I won't be able to wear fashionable clothes. I'll have very few friends because everybody will dislike my appearance. I won't have a boyfriend. I will still be living at home.

### How will I feel in ten years time?

In ten years time I could have serious health problems; I'll have no friends and definitely no husband. As a result of this I won't be able to have a family. I will be alone.

By asking herself these questions, Kate started to feel intense pain. She had started to associate the intense pain of what could happen if she continued to eat too much of the wrong types of food.

However, Kate is not ten years down the line, and so she had the opportunity to change by doing something about her problems right away.

## Step 2 - Creating Positive Leverage

Next, Kate needed to ask herself the following questions so that she could gain positive leverage, i.e. to make herself feel really good.

### How will I feel when I get the result I want?

I will be far more confident and happy. Boys will find me attractive, and all the popular girls will want me to be their friend.

### What must happen to make me feel this way?

Boys must want to take me out. The girls should want me to be a part of their circle. I will want to go abroad and lie on the beach in my bikini. I'll be able to wear fashionable clothes. I will be in control of myself and of my body. I will feel on top of the world.

## Step 3 - Understanding What Your Beliefs Are

Kate needed to understand where her old negative beliefs had come from, and where her new empowering beliefs could take her.

### What is my old negative belief?

I believed that eating would make me feel good and that chocolate could conquer anything. I believed I was overweight and unattractive, and that I had no chance of meeting a nice boy who would take me out. I believed I would never be popular. I believed I would feel ignored and alone.

### What are my new, empowering beliefs?

I now believe food should be used as fuel and not for comfort. I believe I have the strength to lose weight and feel good about myself. I believe I will be happy and enjoy my life.

## Step 4 - Setting the Goal

To achieve her aim, Kate set herself goals that she could work towards. It was important to lay down these specific targets, because they would give her direction.

### What is my ultimate goal?

I want to be able to look good and feel good about myself. I want to lose some weight. I want to be able to love who I am.

### What are my specific goals?

I want to lose two pounds a week until I feel comfortable with my weight and looks. I want to lose 10% of my body fat. I want to be able to go swimming and not feel tired after two lengths of the pool.

## Step 5 - Achieving the Goal

Having goals is crucial but, just as importantly, Kate needed to know how she was going to reach them.

### How will I achieve what I want?

I will ride my bike to school instead of asking Dad for a lift. I am going to swim with my sister on the weekends. I will replace fizzy drinks with water, and chocolate with fruit. I feel that, with a healthy diet and exercise, I can get to where I want to be.

## Step 6 - Action Now

Kate could easily put off taking action. However, there are things that she can do now, immediately. This will encourage her to continue.

**What action can I take now?**

I can tell Dad straight away that I want to ride my bike to school rather than go in the car. I can ask Rachel if I can go swimming with her at the weekend. I will give all my chocolate to mum and ask her to buy more fruit when she next goes shopping.

## Step 7 - Empowering Alternative

Kate needed to empower herself, thereby giving her the courage to continue. Whenever things went wrong she could easily turn back to her old ways, and so alternatives might be required.

**When I feel bad, what will I do?**

When I feel bad I usually eat. With my new strategy, when I feel upset about my situation I will talk to Mum. I will distract myself by doing something active, like swimming.

By following this strategy for change, Kate could understand how her beliefs about food had affected her, and how she would be able to create a new empowering belief to help her lose weight. Kate could now think about the result that she wanted to achieve, and how she was going to get there. Now, if Kate ever feels bad about her situation, she can use one of her alternatives, i.e. speaking to her Mum or doing something active to make herself feel better.

# Visualisation

Once Kate had begun to follow the seven steps to change, asking herself the right questions and using positive language, her next step was visualisation. To do this, you must first be relaxed and then visualise what it is you want, where you want to be and what you want to change. The mind cannot distinguish between vivid imagination and reality; therefore, you need to make the visualisation as real, intense and colourful as possible.

Your sub-conscious mind is a great ally when it comes to visualisation, because it does not make any distinction between reality and fiction. It will actually pick up on your strongest desire, and then organise the facts about this to form them into a plan. So, whatever the material you feed your mind, it will always produce a programme designed to achieve this desire. If you visualise often enough, and give your sub-conscious time to work, you will be amazed at the results.

## The 5 Steps to Visualisation

In order to execute visualisation effectively, it is important to use the right techniques:

### Step One - Find Some Peace and Quiet
If it is difficult to find a quiet space, try using headphones or earplugs. Turn off your mobile phone, and keep distractions to a minimum.

### Step Two - Clear Your Mind
This is a very difficult thing to do, and yet it's very effective. Try and sit without thinking of anything; as a thought comes into your head, imagine it flowing on a river through your mind and out the other side.

### Step Three - Focus
Once your mind is clear, focus on an object in the room - it is quite effective to focus on a stone, charm or candle flame. Once you feel focused, begin visualising.

### Step Four - Appeal to All of Your Senses

It is important to use all of your senses when visualising. What will you see? What will you hear, smell and feel like? What will success taste like?

### Step Five - Relax

The most important part of this process is to relax. Let your mind be your guide through your innermost desires. Relax, and enjoy it.

Kate decided to do this exercise; she found a quiet space to sit and relax. Next, she thought about all the positives that would come from losing the right amount of weight. Kate imagined her family's reaction to her as she walked in the room looking slim, beautiful and elegant; she also visualised being fit and healthy, and able to do well at sports. She imagined walking into school on a bright day, standing with the popular girls who were actually listening to what she had to say. Kate could see herself being the girl she had always wanted to be. By doing this, she felt empowered to take action towards her goal.

Just like programming a computer, you must feed your brain enough information for it to work properly. If Kate could put a lot of effort into her visualisation, she was always more likely to be successful; repetition is a very useful tool when visualising, and if you make visualisation a regular exercise, your Reticular Activating System will kick into action. Each time Kate tells herself that she will be slim, her brain automatically starts trying to find evidence to support her thought. The more she visualises herself as a slim person, the more work her RAS performs to try and prove her right.

## Taking Action

No matter what you decide to do in life, *action is everything* - knowing the way to gain self-belief is only the beginning. How many times have you had a good idea but done nothing about it? Taking action towards your goal may daunt you, or it may excite you. The crucial thing is to do something! Try not to justify why tomorrow is a better day to start something new rather than today.

Many people are afraid of commitment, and find it hard to make decisions. If you take this attitude, the time for action will pass by. In order to be fulfilled, you must make a decision and then take action, with the total commitment and confidence that comes from self-belief. It was all very well Kate adopting the right attitude and knowing exactly what she ought to do, but the real crunch would be the process of transforming everything into some real action.

Kate needed to make decisions, and then to take action. Her first positive step was to eat three regular meals a day, while making sure she cut out the fatty foods; in addition, she started making commitments such as twice-weekly visits to the gym. Whatever the decision she has made to move herself towards her goal, she must continue to take action. It is true that everybody makes mistakes, and inevitably you will make the wrong decision from time to time - this is all part of learning, and the more you practice making decisions, the easier it will become. Take small steps, and one step at a time; follow each step with a celebration. Enjoy your journey.

## Celebrate!

Every small step that Kate takes moves her towards her goal. With every small victory, Kate celebrates - in fact, when she loses a few pounds in weight, she celebrates like there is no tomorrow! Celebration plays a pivotal role in moving towards your goal and changing your beliefs. If you celebrate after every achievement, no matter how insignificant it may seem, then you will encourage yourself to continue along the same path.

Kate is moving closer every day to the person she wants to become; that in itself is worth celebrating. It's a tough journey, but she'll enjoy it and encourage herself in order to progress.

## No Time For Maybe's...

All of us, famous or not, healthy or not, have our own beliefs. Whether these beliefs are positive or negative they are very powerful, and they direct our decisions in life. It is quite true to say that, if you want something enough, you will get it because self-belief can create success.

There are a lot of celebrities who've created their own success through personal confidence. Everybody is capable of creating success through self-belief; in my case, I had the belief that I could get through my illness. Kate's levels of self-belief have already grown, and she's working towards her goal. Whatever your own goal, dream or desire, they are all possible with the right attitude, gratitude and self-belief.

So, if you're thinking "maybe I can, maybe I can't" now is the time to take action. After reading this, you understand the power of self-belief - read the next chapter on positive thinking, and you will find out more about the action you must take in order to make things happen in your life.

> **Raise Your Game Now!**
> *If people can attribute so many, and such a big range of*
> *meanings to just one word, how difficult must it be to make*
> *decisions and communicate effectively in your every day life?*

The subject of language and communication is a vast one, and it's easy to get bogged down in all the psycholinguistics (i.e. the psychology of language). To simplify matters, it's best if you view human language as a set of channels we all have; these enable us to transmit and receive information.

Human beings have evolved into highly complex communicators. You are capable of communicating in many different situations, from face-to-face encounters where you're separated by inches from somebody, to via the telephone, where you could be separated by half the world. You communicate when you can easily be seen, also when you're not visible. You communicate when you talk, but also through your silence. Human beings can communicate in all sorts of different ways, and you as an individual have these various methods at your disposal.

Have you ever wondered why it is that you get on really well with some people, while others are hard to understand? Some people speak really slowly and choose their words precisely, but others talk so fast you haven't a clue what they are saying. Everybody is different; we're all individuals, and everyone has their own mode of communication. We also receive messages from others in different ways.

To explain the concept further, think of it in terms of transmitting radio stations. Some people will be tuned into Radio Four, the frequency where everything is articulate and precise; others prefer Radio One, where they want the latest music and news. Now, the difference between these two stations is not the problem - variety is good - but difficulties could arise if the wavelengths became mixed between transmitting and receiving information. If someone was broadcasting on Radio Four, but you were trying to receive their message on a different frequency - say, the Radio One station - there could be difficulties.

Another way of spotting the differences between communicating styles and methods is to look at the way people speak. Some 'talk' with their hands, while others speak with their heads; despite these differences, effective communication is still possible. The chances of success are governed by your ability to correctly evaluate the person you are communicating with.

Whilst this subject was being discussed in his seminar, a light bulb appeared above Arthur's head. "That's why I have so much trouble communicating with my mother!" he thought. Arthur's mother speaks quietly, slowly and surely; she thinks carefully about her words before spouting forth. On the other hand, Arthur speaks quickly and loudly, sometimes coming out with things he doesn't mean and regrets later. As a consequence, they often fall out with each other, until Arthur phones up his mother – tail between his legs – to apologise for something he may have said without thinking.

## Ways We Communicate

There are *three key ways* in which you can get your message across:

- **What you say**, i.e. the words you use (the 'verbal' system).
- **Your tone**, i.e. how you say the words (the 'prosidic' system).
- **Your physical presence**, i.e. your bearing and gestures (the 'kinesics channel').

In Arthur's job as Manager of a retail outlet, he constantly makes contact with customers. Every day, he has to talk to a variety of different people. It is amazing, Arthur thinks, that he should be capable of talking to all these individuals effectively. The fact is, Arthur doesn't have to think about how he should change his approach towards different people; for him, this happens automatically. He makes changes in the way he communicates without even noticing, once he has evaluated the person he's engaged with. Arthur's speech, tone and physical presence adapts accordingly to the situation. When Arthur has a really nasty individual in his store, he speaks to them completely differently, and acts very differently around them, than he would when dealing with a friendly customer.

Arthur is the type of individual who can make these adjustments naturally, but some people aren't so fortunate. Just as you choose your attitude, you can also select the way in which you communicate with somebody; in Arthur's case, the way he and his colleagues speak to customers is of paramount importance, and it's a factor he used to wish he had more control over. He'd often heard his colleagues speaking to a customer in what he construed as being a rude way – but, they didn't seem to realise they were being offensive when Arthur brought the topic up with them.

## Words, Tone and Body Language

A lot of research has been conducted into what percentages of words, tone and body language influence someone else's behaviour. According to one study, they can be accounted for as follows:

- The words you use account for the smallest portion of your communication - 7%
- Your tone counts for considerably more - 38%
- The way you physically hold yourself makes up the biggest portion of your communication - 55%

This breakdown of how you communicate can be seen in action everyday. For example, if you notice someone fluttering their eyelashes and smiling, you would assume that the conversation they are having is a good one; on the other hand, if you see an individual pointing and looking aggressive while having a conversation, you would think this is not so pleasant. If the nature of the words spoken seems to oppose what the body language is telling you, the message being received could be entirely different again. Therefore, it is true to say that tone and physiology are far more powerful factors than the actual words you use.

## Stalkie's Workout

*Just for fun, say "I love you" really aggressively to your partner, family member or a friend and then note their reaction.*

*Alternatively, the next time you're in a restaurant, say nice things to the manager about the service you've received, also in an aggressive way. Invariably it's your tone and your actions that will get the response.*

Following the seminar, Arthur and his colleagues conducted another exercise to evaluate how the majority of people in their company behaved with customers - the results were startling. However, before trying it out on his colleagues, Arthur decided to test his children first.

Arthur asked his children to pretend that they were being introduced to a really nasty person, and then observed what they said, how they said it and what form their body language took. He then asked them to pretend that they had bumped into someone they were frightened of, and noted once again how they behaved. Finally, he asked them to imagine they were in a poor family, and meeting someone really important who they had to impress because it could lead to their receiving a million pounds a year for life.

Following the experiment, Arthur was pleased to discover that even children change their style of communication when placed in different situations; he also noted that, even if the youngsters did not say anything at all, their different responses to each situation were obvious from the body language used.

When Arthur tried the exercise out on his colleagues, these were the results:

| | Nasty Person | Frightening Person | Important Person |
|---|---|---|---|
| **Words** | Few words said, aggressive, dismissive, scornful, derisory, insulting, no words, nasty, threatening, short, sharp, grunts | Fearful, submissive, cautious, complimentary, 'You look well', 'Wow, you're looking really great!', 'How are you keeping?', respectful | Complimentary, loud, happy, 'Fantastic to see you' |
| **Tone** | Negative, intimidating, monotone, low | Nervous, hesitant, soft tone, quiet | Excited, expressive, energetic, musical |
| **Physical Being** : | Closed, defensive, no eye contact, 'away' gestures, no physical contact, distance, shallow breathing | Bending body, cowering, submissive, open palms, insecure, shaking hands, respectful stance, establishing who's boss, tense facial expression | Open, welcoming, friendly, body contact, hugs, hand shakes, direct eye contact, big breaths, big smiles, sparkling, gestures, energetic |

Following the assessment, Arthur asked his colleagues how they honestly believed they behaved most of the time with customers in store. The majority had to admit that they spoke and behaved as if they were dealing with a nasty person most of the time, i.e. not as they would when trying to impress somebody.

The penny dropped with all of the colleagues; they realised that their body language, lack of words and miserable tone (on occasions) were not giving the right impression to their customers. From that point on, they vowed to Arthur that they would behave and communicate differently.

## Mirroring and Matching

Building a rapport is very important when trying to communicate effectively. Your words and tone go a long way towards building a rapport, but with physiology being 55% of the influence; it's worth knowing how to use your body language for maximum effect.

### Stalkie's Team Workout

*Get yourself into a group of 2, 3 or 4 people.*

*Choose one person in the group to think of an intense feeling they have experienced. It could be related to a wedding, a funeral, the birth of a child, saying goodbye to a loved one – anything will do so long as it involves an intense feeling. Next, get the person to adopt the pose they used at that time.*

*A second person in the group should now mirror the first person exactly, down to the last detail; they need to have every last hair in place, and the exact same facial expressions made. The key to this exercise is to be precise, so don't rush it. When you're done, get any remaining members of the group to check every aspect of the pose, noting every tiny detail – the hands, eye focus, their stance, their fingers and their breathing (this last factor is very important).*

*The person who is mirroring the original pose should now describe what they are feeling - see how close they are to the first person.*

*You will be amazed at the results.*

# When mirroring goes wrong

The surprising strength of this exercise illustrates just how powerful and important your physical being and actions are. They can portray feelings perfectly without a word being said.

Arthur understands how desirable it is for his colleagues to build a rapport with customers by mirroring and matching. They must speak the right words and utter them in the right tone, but they also need to be aware of their body language. Mirroring and matching is an effective technique that Arthur likes his colleagues to use.

In the store, Arthur encourages his colleagues to look at their customers' body gestures and movements as they come through the front doors. The idea is that a colleague can then approach their chosen customer in an identical manner. For example, the colleague could stand in the same way as the customer; if they lean on the desk and are relaxed, then the colleague too should be relaxed and lean on the desk. If the customer sits down to talk, the colleague should also choose to sit down in order to have the conversation. These things are very simple, but they really do help to build a rapport. The same principle goes for adopting identical hand gestures, and alongside this they should try using the same tone of voice, speed, pitch, volume and vocabulary. All of this will make the customer feel valued and well looked after, because they're dealing with someone they like - someone who is just like themselves. Try it, you will be surprised at the results.

Believe it or not, children are the masters of effective communication because they use mirroring and matching techniques without even knowing it. If you see two children having an argument, one child will often report the bad behaviour to a parent with tears in their eyes; when the other child sees this, they too will begin to cry - they will naturally mirror each other's behaviour.

## The Pattern Interrupt

Arthur's colleague Tim faces angry customers every day and as a result, he used to become unhappy as this made him feel inadequate in his dealings with the public. Sometimes, he would take these feelings home; inevitably, his working life affected his home life. Just like Kate, who felt pain when her school friends failed to accept her, Tim also needed to find the source of his pain. That way, he could find new ways to help the situation, since no matter what shop he works in, Tim will always have to face angry customers.

In order to calm them down, Tim needed to build a rapport with his customers. Arthur was taught to mirror and match their actions in order to gain a rapport, but Tim cannot do this in his position; shouting and threatening actions would not go down well with Tim's boss!

Tim now uses another technique, called a pattern interrupt. With this concept, whatever mode the customer is communicating in, Tim tries to do something quite unexpected in order to interrupt their train of thought. The outcome of a pattern interrupt is that it stops a type of behaviour which is ineffective, opening up the possibility of creating a new and more positive direction for the conversation. As an example, you could try asking an outrageous question to change the person's focus - say something not normally acceptable, stupid, funny, confusing etc. You could also try using your physical being to 'pattern interrupt', through body movement, facial expressions, speed of movement etc. The aim is to introduce a new element to the conversation so that the person is interrupted and unable to continue with their original line of argument.

As an example, let's imagine that a customer is shouting at Tim because the product he bought does not work - they are becoming quite frustrated. Tim could try a pattern interrupt like this:

**Customer:** "I have just about had enough of your company - this is the third time I've come to you with a faulty television set!"

**Tim:** "Oh right - what is your favourite TV programme?"

**Customer:** "What has that got to do with my television not working?"

Now, Tim has managed to successfully interrupt his customer's train of thought, because he has responded to Tim's unexpected question.

**Tim:** "You look like the sort of person who is interested in sports, and at the moment we are doing free set-top boxes."

The customer has now thought about something completely different to the subject that was making him angry, thus lessening his emotional state. Quite simply, all Tim has done is to ask them a question; now, the angry person has to stop and think of an answer, making them forget the next line of their argument! The brain finds it difficult to focus on two things at once, hence the customer cannot concentrate on being angry and answering the questions. Tim chose to ask a confusing question, and this interrupted his customer's pattern.

In his home life, Tim now uses other extreme methods to interrupt his girlfriend's pattern. When they have an argument and Tim wants to calm the situation down, he suddenly behaves crazily, barking like a dog and pulling a funny face. Not only does his girlfriend stop mid-flow - inevitably, she laughs. The whole situation is instantly defused.

Back at work, once Tim has cleverly interrupted the angry customer's pattern, he starts to mirror them. If they speak softly to him, Tim speaks softly back, because doing this puts the customer at ease. He continues his conversation by choosing the same type of vocabulary that they use. Tim finds that, when mirroring customers as precisely as possible, he enjoys the best results. It was a difficult thing to do when he first started the job, but the more angry customers he got, the easier it became. Now, Tim does not even realise he is doing it.

This process of interrupting someone's pattern, then mirroring and matching them, can also work when a person is sad. Firstly, you could ask a question just as Tim did or, even better, try acting sadder than they are. Their reaction may be that they want to help you – in this way, you have efficiently reversed the situation. Naturally, this will take their mind off their own problems. To do this well, try speaking in a low pitch with a monotone voice, and have your head and shoulders down, breathing in a very shallow way.

There are many different ways you can use pattern interrupts, but the crux is to get the conversation back under your control. Obviously, this technique improves with practice. Try it out at home first with family and friends, then use it at the pub or supermarket. Eventually, you will feel confident enough to try it at work.

## Female Intuition

Arthur discovered (as most men do!) that Mary, being a woman, has something called 'female intuition'. This is because overall, women are far more perceptive than men. If we describe someone as 'perceptive' or 'intuitive', we are usually referring to his or her ability to read another person's body language. When Arthur comes home from the pub with Ryan and tells Mary that he only had one drink, she gets a gut feeling that he is lying - this usually means that Arthur has said something which does not agree with his body language, and Mary can pick up on that very easily. Apart from their ability to pick up on body language, another reason for 'female intuition' relates to the things they do when they become mothers. During the early years of childhood, a mother relies almost solely on non-verbal communication to care for her child; it gives them plenty of practice in reading 'non-verbal' communication.

Children's body language is more pronounced than that of adults, and they can find it difficult to get away with even a simple lie. Mary notices this with her youngest son, James; when she asks him if he has cleaned his teeth before going to school, he says "yes." James then instantly covers his mouth with his hands. This is an automatic response, and it quite clearly indicates to Mary that he his lying. Such a bold gesture can easily be read by his mother.

## Reading Body Language

You use body language all the time, although you are not always conscious of it. Moreover, you tend to notice other peoples' changes in body language more than you do your own. Frequently, your perception of other people will help you to understand their feelings towards a situation. Body language is an outward reflection of a person's emotional condition; every gesture or movement that you make can indicate an emotion that you're feeling at any given time.

Take the example of Kate - when she sat down in a social environment, she immediately smoothed her skirt down to cover her lower area. We know that Kate is very self-conscious about her weight, and in particular she believed that her thighs were far too big. How do we deduce this from her body language?

The key to reading this type of body language is to listen to what the person is saying while also taking notice of their emotional condition by looking at the coordinating body movements. In this case, if Kate was having dinner out with her friends, she might say: "I am just going to have a salad - I'm not that hungry" while at the same time smoothing her skirt down. A conclusion could be that Kate did not want to eat too much as she thought she was overweight already.

# Use Your Body

Research into body language has revealed that, if you alter your body language, you can change many things relating to your approach to life.

Kate became worried every time she was invited to go out with her friends; she would fret about what to wear, and whether she looked 'fat'. She would stand with her shoulders slumped, her voice was quiet and she used her arms to cover her stomach. Kate's body language indicated her lack of confidence. If she could change her stance - i.e. by standing tall, using her arms to make friendly gestures and leaving those arms well away from her stomach, not only would she feel more confident in herself, but she would become more likeable to others.

When changing your body language, you'll communicate differently with the people around you; in turn, they will interact differently with you. As you increase your awareness of body language, you may become self-conscious, and aware of all your expressions - prepare to be amazed at how many gestures you do actually make.

You can't escape body language, so use it to help you. Flash your teeth, keep your chin up and mirror others.

# Our Five Senses

Effective communication relies on many different components, all of which make up the influencing power of the messages you are trying to convey. You know and understand that there are three main elements which make up your communication: what you say, how you say it and your body language - each of these factors can effect the message being received. In addition to these elements, you also have another set of influences, these being your five senses:

■ Sight (*visual*)

- Touch (*kinaesthetic*)
- Sound (*auditory*)
- Smell (*olfactory*)
- Taste (*gustatory*)

  Although you do not typically use your smell and taste senses to communicate in modern society, these are still of great significance, and have been used to assist communication throughout history. For example, if you smell alcohol on a man in the local bus shelter at 10.00am, he is instantly communicating the type of person he is. Or, if you've ever kissed someone in a club who tastes of cigarettes, they instantly communicate to you that they are a smoker!

  Although these two senses do play a part in our communication, they're not the most used. It is the three remaining ones - touch, sound and sight - that play the largest roles. However, they won't be used in equal measure, and you will always have one predominant sense that you use to communicate with. In short, you may rely on either your *visual*, *kinaesthetic* or *auditory* senses to get the message across.

## Visual

Arthur is a very visual person. He appreciates art, and loves to watch plays at the theatre. Favourite colours for Arthur are bright yellow and brilliant red; he firmly believes in the phrase 'a picture paints a thousand words'. Communicating effectively with Arthur would involve putting the emphasis on art, style and designs – these would really get his juices flowing.

## Kinaesthetic

On the other hand, Arthur's mother is a person who relies upon her feelings. She 'feels' her words out, and always goes with her gut reactions, no matter what she can see or hear. More often than not, she is very softly spoken and articulate; these are all characteristics of a person whose dominant sense is kinaesthetic. Meaningful communication with Arthur's mum would include talking slowly, and it would be important to carefully think about, and plan, your sentences and choice of words – this would build a great rapport.

## Auditory

Ryan, Arthur's brother, is a very auditory person. Those like Ryan who have sound as their key sense are far more difficult to spot. He is very articulate with his language, and he appreciates the way things sound. Ryan enjoys loud music, and loves listening; someone with a 'musical' voice would be the type of person he would enjoy talking to. Using phrases such as 'how does that sound to you?' would help form lines of effective communication with Ryan.

These people have very different characters, with alternative ways of communicating. Unfortunately, this used to be a recipe for disaster where Arthur and his mother were concerned - however, Arthur is now aware of these differences, and he's able to communicate much more productively with her. Moreover, he's taught his colleagues in the store about these differences between people. At first they thought Arthur was having a laugh, but then they turned the exercise into a game and started trying to spot the diverse characters among themselves; next, the colleagues learnt to identify these traits in their customers.

Soon enough, Arthur's staff began to realise that when selling to a visual person, they needed to use phrases such as 'how does that look to you?' and 'is that how you see yourself?' They also learnt to focus on the look and style of each product. With kinaesthetic people, they started to talk about how a product feels; a colleague would ask their customer to touch the item, and try it out. As for those identified as being auditory in nature, the staff would now use words and phrases that appealed to that particular sense, e.g. 'does that click with you?' and 'can you hear the difference?' or 'how does that sound?' It was great fun to try out the different styles – but more importantly, it worked! By transmitting to customers on the same wavelength they were receiving on, a rapport would be built, whereupon the colleagues could influence the buying decisions. Sales began to climb!

# Male and Female Communication

When it comes to communication, men and women are fundamentally different. No, one is not better than the other - they are just different. You should also realise there are differences in how men and women learn, and the ways in which they affect each other. Generally speaking, men tend to be concerned with outcomes; if there is a problem, they will only want to know the solution to it. Women, on the other hand, tend to be more creative. They are interested in discussions and sharing, and they want to be respectful of other people's needs. Of course, this is generalising – there are shades of grey here, just as you would find with all the differences between men and women's personality traits. There will be women who are outcome oriented, and men who like to discuss and share.

Arthur decided he wanted to take the family away for a really good holiday to the Bahamas. He looked at the budget to see how long it would take him to save for the break, and then went on the internet to view the accommodation types, available dates and so on. Next, Arthur went to the local travel agent and picked up some brochures - only then did he sit down with Mary to approach the subject.

After putting in the effort to get that far, Arthur was feeling very pleased with himself. However, Mary thought he'd been very rude, organising all this without even discussing it with her. Mary felt left out. She thought Arthur could at least have had the simple courtesy to include her in sorting out their family holiday. Two completely different viewpoints - one family.

Communication difficulties between men and women not only occur in the home, but also within business. The majority of women will tend to share everything, and want to let everyone know what is happening; most men will just want to get on with it. This can cause huge conflicts within a company. A woman at board level will want to discuss a situation in the business before even thinking of a solution - her fellow, male director may take the opinion that she's being ineffective, through not coming up with a solution immediately. Meanwhile, the female director may believe that he is ineffective because he's apparently reached a decision without knowing all the facts. Of course, they may both be right, and a compromise might be the best way forward. A man could be under the impression that he has found the solution, but it might well be the case that the problems are found only when the decision is communicated – some discussion beforehand would probably have been appropriate. Respect for each other, and the efficiency with which they work together, can be reduced purely and simply because they have different approaches to a problem.

In personal relationships, male and female communication is obviously paramount, but conflict often arises when women and men approach a situation differently. Understanding why this is, and appreciating the fact that differences can be worked around, will go some way towards alleviating any problems that may arise.

Communication affects every area of our lives. Whether male or female, your communication skills need to be just as effective. Remember that it's not what we say, but the way in which all three aspects of communication work together - words, tone and body language – that counts. No matter what the situation may be, meaningful communication is life affirming.

"Why haven't you already done something about that thing that I've never mentioned till now!?"

# The Third Round
## *Make a Friend*

### 11 Me Tarzan, You Jane!

**It sounds like a radical notion, but aside from the fact that we both come from the same species, men and women are totally different. Now, you may well be aware of this fact, but surprisingly few of us are willing to admit it. As John Gray says in his famous series of books, we are on separate planets, i.e. Mars and Venus; we come down to earth sometimes, but then forget that we come from other planets. Of course, the degree of disparity between us varies from man to man and woman to woman, but disparities there are - the way in which we cope with these dictates how we get along together both in society and our relationships.**

These differences mean that communication with the opposite sex on all levels is fundamental to our survival. A lack of understanding and communication between the sexes has produced a worrying statistic: approximately 50% of all marriages end in divorce. Men and women are different - nothing can change that, but they are able to improve their understanding of each other. When you do understand and learn to love the differences, it's like opening a new emotional bank account. As you invest the interest grows, and you start to reap the rewards. Nice things start happening when you have brilliant relationships at home and at work, and as a result, you live longer and lead a healthier life.

163

Following his change in attitude after the motivational seminar, both Arthur's work and home life seem to have advanced a great deal. Working on his communication skills has been of paramount importance in Arthur's change of attitude. A crucial element in the art of effective communication is knowing and understanding the different behaviours that people have; Arthur wanted to work on his relationship with Mary even further, so he booked two tickets for a seminar about understanding the sexes.

There are obvious differences between men and women; some you notice and expect to see everyday. When the family go out to dinner, it is not unusual for Mary, Hannah and Patsy to end up in the bathroom together. For the women it is a social thing, checking their hair and make-up whilst having a chat. However, the girls tend to assume that, when Arthur heads to the gents, he is going for one obvious reason. How shocked would Mary be if Arthur piped up: "Jack, I'm off to the bathroom, do you want to come with me?"

During the 60's and 70's, there were action groups who made it their sole aim to persuade the world that men and women were equal, and hence should be treated the same. There is no doubt that both sexes should be given the same opportunities in order to maximise their potential, but we are not the same in terms of our innate abilities – we are equal, but different.

## The Way We're Wired

Men and women evolved differently, because they had to. Simply put, early men were hunters and gatherers; women were gatherers too, but they also had to be homemakers and child carers. In short, the men protected, and women nurtured. Our brains and bodies have been designed according to these various job roles and hence they are very different, simply because they've needed to function in alternate ways. For example, men needed to have a good sense of direction because, having killed their prey, they would need to track back home. Moreover, good spatial abilities were indispensible, because a man needed to take aim at his prey - that's why men are so good at reading maps. In their role, back in the cave looking after the family, women had no need to develop a map-reading ability; instead, they developed other skills more suited to their own roles, such as that of multi-tasking. Women can do more than one thing at a time, because looking after children requires that skill.

Evolution has given men and women many contrasting skills and abilities - a number of these are puzzling at first glance. I bet you recognise the following foibles associated with the sexes:

Men can't find things; they will stand by the wardrobe insisting that their best shirt isn't in there, until a woman (i.e. the wife or girlfriend) comes along and picks it out without a second glance. This is because women developed wider peripheral vision for their nurturing role, plus an attention to detail that men did not need in their role as hunter. They didn't need to find things in the cave – that's what women were for!

Meanwhile, women can't park their car in a tight space, due to their inferior spatial ability. Although they are able to learn the task in order to pass their driving tests, changing conditions of light, distance, and surrounding traffic mean that they continue to find parking difficult.

When a woman asks for more attention, there is the characteristic, totally blank look on her male partner's face – he may have just washed her car, bought her a new kettle and even taken the rubbish out to the dustbin, and yet she still requires more affection! For a man, showing emotion often equales to being out of control (he'll have heard the phrase 'big boys don't cry') and he simply doesn't understand a woman's need for constant displays of affection.

We all know the teenage girl who's straight on the phone when she arrives home to chat for two hours to the best friend she's just left. Yes, women like to talk; it's how they're made. Their speech and language skills are far more developed than a man's. A woman's brain is set up differently, and it is this which gives them the facility.

See if this one rings any bells: A couple drive along for hours, with the man not being able to say exactly where they are (insisting they're not lost), but still refuses to ask for directions. In his eyes, asking for advice equates to losing control. However, for a woman, stopping to ask someone for guidance could open up a whole new conversational opportunity, whilst providing the chance to solve a difficult problem - hence, she will not hesitate to do it.

All of the above represent typical situations caused by the distinct ways in which men and women's brains have evolved. However, we should note that although typical, they are not compulsory. Some women are experts at reverse parallel parking, and there are men who love to chat. Naturally, there are exceptions to every rule!

When Hannah discovered she would be giving birth to twin boys, she bought the things that little boys should have. She decorated the nursery in blue, bought them wooden trains, and sought out clothes with pictures of cars on them. Similarly, when the family found out that Hannah was having boys, they purchased blue blankets and little dungarees. You would probably do the same without even thinking about it. This is down to social conditioning, i.e. what you have been brought up to believe is the right thing to do. Another example of social conditioning can be seen when you attend a funeral; the emotion that you need to display is one of sorrow, sadness, and condolence - our actions are designed to display this. You wear black, have a sombre face, and you cry. This is, we believe, the right way to behave at a funeral. Our feelings of sorrow will usually be genuine of course, but it is the way in which we display these emotions that can be seen as part of a social training programme.

With regard to our knowledge of gender differences, times are changing. Until recently, a newborn baby was treated as a blank canvas, upon which parents and teachers could paint preferences for them during the early years; however, there is now biological evidence to show it is the way our brains are wired, plus our hormones, that are responsible for the way we think.

At the seminar Arthur and Mary attended they were taught that, whether you are male or female, it is the way your brain is wired rather than external influences that decides who you are. The nature/nurture debate is one that's always interested Mary, being a schoolteacher. Although you cannot have one without the other, Mary began to think about the nature aspect more than she had ever done before.

Mary is well aware that men are generally not great conversationalists. She often thinks Arthur is being rude when he does not respond to her in very much detail; in contrast to this, Arthur gets frustrated with Mary when she asks "how has your day been - what have you been doing?" when he just wants space to relax. That is one of the reasons why Mary really enjoys having a chat with Patsy; she always seems to get far more out of the conversation. It's no secret that women love to chat, and in comparison to men, they are experts. There are many reasons why this should be - for a start, girls tend to start talking at a much earlier age than boys. More importantly, the female brain has a specific area for speech.

This part of a woman's brain is primarily located in the front of the left hemisphere, but there's also a small speech section in the right hemisphere. With an area devoted entirely to speech on both sides of the brain, it is no wonder that females are such great conversationalists. The fact that women have specific areas to deal with speech means that the rest of the brain is available to do other things, giving them the power to multi-task.

## 'Why Men Don't Listen and Women Can't Read Maps'...

Women are great at chatting and they love to talk, especially at the end of the day. In their book 'Why Men Don't Listen and Women Can't Read Maps', Allan and Barbara Pease state that on average, women use approximately

20,000 words, sounds and gestures a day to communicate, whereas men can only manage about 7,000. So, it's not uncommon for a woman to have a lot more left when the evening comes around. Women gain a lot of comfort through talking about everything that's happened during the day, whereas men often want to just keep quiet. It is not difficult to see how this can lead to problems. During Arthur and Mary's seminar, the women were asked to think of an occasion when they had felt as though their partner was not listening to them; Mary told Arthur that when she comes in from work, she likes to talk about what has happened during the day. The men were then asked to give their feedback, whereupon Arthur made it clear to Mary that he likes to come in from work and have a little time of peace and relaxation. In short, he needs some 'Arthur' time after a hard, long day.

Mary does not want to deliberately disturb Arthur's quiet evening; talking is just her way of dealing with things. Her head is wired very differently to Arthur's, because male brains are organised into compartments, and this

gives them the ability to separate and store information. Therefore at the end of the day, Arthur can file everything away. He does not want to talk about anything until he's thought things through - to him, this is a sensible way forward. The female brain does not store information in this way; problems keep going around in a woman's head. Hence to get rid of matters that are troubling her, Mary talks about them.

## The Art of Inter-Gender Communication

When it comes to relationships, getting the communication right is key. For this you need to remember three points:

**1** When talking to a man, keep it direct and to the point. There must be a clear outcome - not just talking for the sake of it. Give a male just one thing to think about at a time. If you multi-track subjects (and on top of multi-tracking, go around the houses a bit), men get lost and stop paying attention.

This difference causes problems not just at home, but at work too. A man could lose confidence in his female colleague because, to his mind, she just wants to chat instead of coming up with solid solutions. This could be perceived by the male as a lack of ability, especially if he's not paid much attention to the variances in male and female communication styles, and their needs.

**2** When a woman talks at the end of the day, she does not want or need interruptions. She is fulfilling a biological need to talk, not just for the love of it, but because she needs to share and include you in her life. This will help her to feel valued, and understood. A bit of friendly advice for all the men out there (and I must credit John Gray for this information): you are not expected to respond. The golden rule is that no solutions are required. Don't, whatever you do, try to take control and offer a solution - this will aggravate the situation. You simply need to look in the woman's direction and actively listen by nodding, agreeing and making the right noises (ahs and ums), sound sympathetic at appropriate moments, and give compliments when they are needed. Now, you're probably thinking 'okay, what's in it for me?' Well, your lady will feel more love for you. Actively listening is one of the most romantic things a man can do.

**3** In working environments, a female boss dealing with a problem will often chat about it before coming up with a solution. This is not a weakness - it's just how they are so, guys, please listen and contribute politely. If you're a male boss and have a lot of women working for you, then you must listen and go along with it - you can't stop nature taking its course. It's all about respecting the differences.

Men often get into trouble in relationships when their women are indirect. Patsy tried to gain her love from Simon negatively, and she didn't get the result she wanted, largely because he was completely unaware of her hidden agenda. The conversation went something like this:

**Simon:** "Shall we go out for dinner tonight, Patsy?"
**Patsy:** "I don't mind - can if you want to."
**Simon:** "Excellent, I've already booked us a table at the Capitol Pizzeria."
**Patsy:** "Oh, I don't like that restaurant. Do we have to?"
**Simon:** "No, darling; it doesn't matter, we'll go some other time, and somewhere else."

To Simon this conversation was very simple - his wife does not like the restaurant he picked, and so they would choose not to go there. For Patsy however, this conversation was a lot more complex; she wanted to sound unconcerned about going out with her husband. In this way, she hoped to push him into saying just how much he wanted to spend time with her, because he loves her. Patsy also aspired to encourage her husband to change the venue because she doesn't like it, as a gesture to show how much he loves her.

Very often, men complain that they are expected to be mind readers; women feel that men are insensitive. The truth of the situation, however, is that women's brains are process-orientated, that is they enjoy the process of communicating. Men find such a lack of structure and purpose very frustrating. In business, this indirect speech can be a real problem for women, because men find their conversation hard to follow, potentially leading to the rejection of perfectly sound proposals.

Arthur learnt in the seminar that indirect speech is part of a woman's internal wiring. In order to build a more successful relationship with Mary, he would need to listen effectively and sincerely by using good 'listening sounds' and body language. To make an impact when communicating with a man, Mary learnt, you need to set up an agenda. She should tell Arthur what she wanted to talk about and when, the expected duration of the meeting and, most importantly, the desired result of the chat. By doing this, Mary would be appealing to Arthur's logical mind. Direct speech is the way men do business.

Communication is not the only area where men and women differ. Their expectations of a relationship vary widely too, as explained below.

Female desires in a relationship - they want their partners to be caring, loving, romantic listeners, flower-buying, protecting, complimentary, understanding, secure, reliable, fun, spontaneous, sympathetic, adoring, worshipping, devoted, irresistible, passionate, tender, starry-eyed, sensitive, kind, thoughtful, gentle, helpful, considerate, compassionate, concerned, perceptive, appreciative, protecting, dependable, trustworthy, entertaining and exciting. And as if that wasn't enough, they want their men to never see any fat bits, and never to offer a solution.

In contrast, men could be said to have just one desire in a relationship - that their woman turns up naked!

Now, I know this is only a joke but as the saying goes, many a true word is spoken in jest, and there are some elements of truth here. Let's take a look at a few more proven differences to see how this can be.

## Attitudes and Emotions

Men and women perceive the world through very different eyes. On the one hand, men take note of objects and their relationship to one another; this relates to their need to hit a target back in those hunting days. Meanwhile, women literally see the bigger picture - they see the fine detail. Colours are a good example: a male sees blue, where a female may see cobalt, lilac, navy, sapphire, indigo, powder blue and so on. Men are concerned with getting results, achieving goals, power and status. Women focus on communication and co-operation. These peculiarities lead to different emotions between a man and woman, and how they deal with their feelings differs too.

Emotions can get in the way of many fruitful relationships. As you might expect, emotion is a tricky area of the brain to pinpoint; generally speaking for men, it lies in the right side, which means that it can operate separately from other functions. Hence, a man can put emotion to one side in most circumstances. For women, emotion is more widespread, being located in both sides of the brain - this affects the way in which they deal with situations.

This difference is very clearly demonstrated by male and female attitudes to sex. A woman, in the main, has to feel emotionally attached to her partner, and she needs to feel loved and cared-for before she will consider an intimate relationship. In contrast to this, a man is ready in a minute or so, without demanding any emotional attachment. This is why the sex industry caters almost exclusively for men through lap dancing bars, massage parlours, and phone sex etc.

If there is an emotional issue to be discussed in the Collins household, Mary, Kate and Rachel are usually comfortable with this; while talking about it, they sometimes become emotional themselves. Men are much less likely to do this, indeed Arthur has been known to refuse a discussion. Arthur, like many men, tends to hide his emotions - this is due to the ancient idea that talking about feelings shows weakness. Men are naturally suspicious, controlled and competitive. Becoming emotional, for a man, means being out of control and feeling vulnerable.

Being in control is a male requirement, and this is why a lot of them find it hard to take advice. Seeking the wisdom of others is seen as a weakness - strong men tend to sort things out for themselves. When Ryan decided to reduce his smoking, he wanted to do it on his own because as a man, he needed to feel as though he was capable of solving his own problem. Mary tried to discuss Ryan's problem with him, and wanted to know how he was feeling about everything; Ryan saw this as criticism. Of course, Mary was an innocent victim in this situation because she just wanted to help. Unfortunately, Ryan took this as a sign that she considered him weak. Most men find it difficult to openly discuss their problems and feelings.

In contrast, women discuss their problems and feelings all the time. When Mary talks, she gains comfort and relief from the process. This is the nub of the problem, because men work out their feelings in their head; if a problem presents itself to Arthur, he will remain quiet while using the right side of his brain to find a solution. Because the male brain can only cope with one task at a time, men often find it difficult to solve problems and talk about them at the same time.

## "But **why** won't you have a pointless argument with me?"

## Men Don't Stand a Chance

The instinct we call 'female intuition' is actually a woman's ability to notice the tiniest of details, plus their aptitude when it comes to registering the smallest of changes in someone's appearance or character. This is a phenomenon that's always baffled men. Arthur never ceases to be amazed at the way in which his wife can spot everything when she is scanning a room at a party, or when he has something to hide. And yet, when it comes to backing the car into their garage, she can't see a thing!

This is not just a myth aimed at unfairly criticising women. Judging the distance between the car bumper and the garage wall is a spatial skill that women are not very good at; men are better at this, because they still have those hunting skills that were honed when a man had to judge the distance, speed and size of a potential kill. However, when it comes to protecting the family, women are best, because it was their job to shield the young from predators. In times gone by, it was essential that women were able to pick up on the slightest changes in the behaviour of their children because these might indicate hunger, injury etc.

During the seminar, Arthur learned about other factors related to vision and perception. He was fascinated to discover that women have a wider peripheral vision than men; once again, the reasons for this go back to the functions they had to fulfil in ancient times. In order to defend her family, a woman's brain software allows her to see clearly 45 degrees either side of her head, plus above and below her nose. Men, on the other hand, are programmed to see targets at a distance. They have a sort of 'tunnel vision', meaning they can only see clearly when looking directly in front of themselves.

This wider peripheral vision is a useful tool for a woman to have. Jack is well aware that Hannah can see everything; she always moans at him for looking at other women. On the other hand, Hannah is very rarely accused of checking out other men. The truth of the matter is, Hannah looks at men just as much as Jack looks at women, but due to her superior peripheral vision she rarely gets caught.

Women have many other tools that men worry about – an example would be 'mother's instinct'. Mothers are great at spotting a variety of emotions in their children, and they can detect the smallest of changes to a baby's cry. This talent is not limited to detecting changes in children's behaviour though; yes, that's right, women can also pick up on the slightest alterations to a man's behaviour. In a face-to-face situation, e.g. when Hannah confronts Jack about looking at other women, Jack finds it very difficult to convince his partner that he's innocent. This is because Hannah is extremely good at picking up on body language. Women have slightly superior sensory equipment, and this enables them to effectively translate verbal, visual and other signals. Most men find it hard to lie to a woman.

Clearly, Hannah does not have special, super senses – it's just that, by comparison, Jack's have been dulled. In Hannah's world, she expects Jack to read not only her verbal signals, but also her body language too; she wants him to anticipate her needs. For evolutionary reasons, men like Jack are not wired in this way, and so he finds it hard to live up to these expectations.

## Nature versus Nurture

As I've already stated, men and women evolved very differently, and this is reflected in their respective strengths and weaknesses. Men, who were responsible for hunting, developed skills in long distance navigation, the forming of tactics to obtain their goal, and skills to hit a target. They did not require good conversational skills, nor did they have to worry about being sensitive to anyone's emotional needs. For their part, women needed the ability to perform several tasks at one time, and effective communication skills were essential. Our brains have evolved according to these requirements.

One of Arthur's very best friends, John, went travelling for a long period of his life. Christmas is a great time of year in the Collins household, and John loves to entertain the family by telling stories about his travels. Every year, John's narrative becomes more exciting and even more amazing - this last Christmas was no different. John tells a story related to the time he spent living in a small village in Iowa, U.S.A. While there he made some great friends, and among them was one unique couple.

Before telling his story, John would explain that, when he was younger, parents used to raise their kids with the idea that each child was identical at birth – almost like a blank canvas, upon which a personality could be created by significant others. Now, John explains, there are scientists who've discovered evidence to the contrary. Today, there is a general consensus that you are who you are, because of your genes.

John says that his friend in Iowa, Bob, had to go through a routine circumcision whilst very young. Unfortunately there was a complication, which resulted in the amputation of his penis. Bob's parents were distraught; they felt it would be awkward for him to grow up with such a severe deformity. Their decision was to bring their child up as if he were a girl. To that end, they gave Bob dolls and teddy bears, and dressed him in pink; even though Bob grew up as a 'she', it became apparent that he was not a happy child. John felt sad to say that Bob made almost no friends at school, and he hadn't wanted to go out – not surprisingly, Bob became very depressed during his teenage years.

The problem became so unbearable, John explained, that Bob's parents finally decided to tell him everything. He was not angry, as you might have expected – instead, the confused teenager was very relieved. Bob immediately conducted research into the situation to see what could be done; this led to surgery that reconstructed his penis. Now, Bob is a very happily married man. John always finishes the story with a smile as he explains the moral - you cannot change fundamental things about the way you were born through enforcing an alternative upbringing.

In the opinion of scientists, the balance of nature versus nurture tips in the favour of nature. Men and women are different, and we cannot change that; you are who you are, because you were born that way.

While we're looking at the nature v. nurture debate, we should consider why some men and women are gay. They could be seen to go against all of this research about typical male and female abilities but, as we shall see, what happens to them before birth dictates their make-up. Our male/female characteristics are formed in the womb; we all start off with a basically female configuration (that's why men have nipples), but somewhere around six to eight weeks into the pregnancy, male hormones are delivered to the foetus. The quantity of these hormones can vary, with the amount dictating the overall sex of the baby, it's male/female characteristics, and what the sexual orientation will be. Scientific evidence behind this disproves the theory that being gay is a choice to be made – it's fixed before birth, and the upbringing a child receives will not change that. It also explains why some women have male abilities, e.g. being able to parallel park, and why some men can do typically female things, like communicating efficiently.

## The Commitment Thing

The concept of one man and one woman living together has formed the core of our society for a very long time. Are there any advantages to marriage? For men, in evolutionary terms, there are no benefits; they have a drive to spread their seed as far, wide and as often as they can. Despite this fact, the majority of men still marry. Women, on the other hand, have a drive to create a home that will enable them to bring up their children in safety, hence they do not normally have a need for more than one partner/father. So, men and women view marriage from different perspectives. Men may see the advantages in having their meals prepared for them, and a regular sex life but for women, it's all about security and feeling wanted. Being in a relationship is essential to most women, since it makes them feel special.

The word 'commitment' provokes fear in most men. When younger, Jack felt like that whenever he was faced with the possibility of a long-term relationship; he would get cold feet, and start to worry about missing out. Jack thought single life was all about going out with your mates and meeting attractive women - all those opportunities would slip by if he were tied down. In truth, when Jack was single, he spent most nights in front of the TV with a take-away on his own. Men worry that commitment equals missing out.

In Arthur's seminar, he used the example of his brother-in-law, and the speaker empathised. Arthur discovered it was not Jack's fault; he was not aiming to be bad at commitment, it's just the way in which he is wired. On the other hand, Arthur now realises, to be true to one person is a priority in a woman's mind.

For both Arthur and Mary, the seminar was invaluable. Now, they feel they understand each other much better, and realise why they sometimes don't see eye to eye. As a result, Arthur and Mary respect and value each other more than they've ever done before.

## Future Perfect?

When we all lived in caves, our roles in life were easy to understand and everyone just got on with their jobs. No one ever expected a man to communicate better, or a woman to learn navigational skills. He wasn't expected to help with the chores in the cave, and she wasn't expected to go out and kill lunch. This precise demarcation of male/female roles made things easy to understand. Nowadays, things are different. There are all sorts of demands made upon both men and women.

Over the centuries, not much has changed for the majority of men; most still go out to work in order to provide for their families. However, we do now have so-called 'modern men' who stay at home and look after the children. For modern women, however, many of their priorities have changed. These days, they have professional careers, money, prestige and power. As the years have progressed, both men and women's brains have evolved in order to cope with modern society, and continual minor adjustments have been made. This is the way of evolution - but maybe these evolutionary alterations have not kept pace with the changes in expectations that our society has.

Men and women are different - not better or worse, just different. This is proven by science, and yet political correctness still tries to deny it. There remains a strong belief that men and women should be treated in exactly the same way, perpetuated by those under the delusion that men and women are the same.

The long and short of it is, relationships between men and women do work, even though there are huge contrasts between the sexes. A lot of the time, in business, I think the polarity between men and women can actually be the strength of an organisation. Using the very best qualities of both genders is often a recipe for success. In my opinion, you have to credit women for their fantastic ability to manage a family successfully, and for their organisational skills in the workplace. Men have great qualities too, thanks to those primeval hunting instincts, but these take a different form; the fact is, we all need to learn about each other and respect and embrace the differences in order to prosper. Of course, there is always room for improvement, and many men will have to learn and acknowledge a bit more about themselves, and about women for that matter, in order to survive in the modern world. And yes, women need to do the same.

Raise
Your
GAME
Now!

# The Third Round
## *Make a Friend*

### 12 Needs and Deeds

**Like you, Arthur now understands that a lot of his decisions and the resulting deeds are based on how people communicate using their words, tone and body language. However, looking beyond what you can see and hear is just as important in your decision making. Decisions are made and actions are taken every day - lots of them. Occasionally, these decisions are major ones - some even life changing - but mostly, our decisions are small ones. You decide what to eat for breakfast, what to wear, how to respond to partners or children; each and every one of these decisions is based on your needs, and the needs of those around you.**

Kate may decide to eat a low-fat breakfast, because she is worried about her appearance and wants to lose weight. Arthur decides to put on his smartest suit to impress the Area Manager. Hannah decides to respond quickly to the needs of her twins. Ryan decides not to drink alcohol anymore because that's when he's most likely to light up a cigarette. Each of these decisions is made to meet a human need.

## What Are Needs?

The decisions you make and the deeds that they lead to, are all related to the needs you have to fulfil in your daily life. In order to understand how this works, let's look at the basic human needs as distilled by prominent psychologists, particularly the ones that have made a difference to my way of thinking and, I hope, will make a difference to your way of thinking too.

Most authors of major self-improvement books have identified the needs that everybody has to meet to ensure happiness. Abraham Maslow is one of the most famous: A humanistic psychologist, he was best known for his 'hierarchy of needs':

### 1 Biological and physiological (our body's needs)

These are the most basic needs, i.e. food, drink, shelter, warmth, air to breathe and sleep.

### 2 Safety (being secure)

You need to have protection from the elements, plus security, law, order and stability.

### 3 Belonging and love

A very powerful need. You need to belong to groups, whether it is in a work situation, in a family, or friendship. Also, you need affection via relationships.

### 4 Esteem (what you think about yourself)

This is your perception of yourself, and what you believe others think about you. This need includes self-esteem and your need for independence, status, dominance, prestige and achievement. Being given responsibility at work or in the family may satisfy this.

### 5 Self-actualisation (growth, learning)

Here, we're talking about reaching your true potential. You need self-fulfilment, and to seek personal growth and improvement.

This hierarchy helps us to understand how our most basic needs motivate us. Maslow's model proposed that basic needs, such as hunger and thirst, must be satisfied before higher needs such as esteem and self-actualisation can be achieved. So if, for example, you're having difficulty breathing, your are unlikely to be worried about your sales target for that month. Similarly, if you're homeless, self-actualisation will not be important to you.

An appreciation of this principle is vital when dealing with others, and understanding the decisions they take. As a store manager, Arthur has a difficult job; if he notices that a member of his team is under-performing and not taking part in team activities, it may be because they are distracted by their failure to meet their need for shelter - maybe their home is being repossessed, for example. In this instance, Arthur's job as manager is to help his colleague meet this basic physiological and biological need before he can expect anything more from them in the store.

I am sure most of you know someone (maybe even yourself?) that has 'thrown a sickie' from work when in reality they've stayed at home feeling

sorry for themselves about a problem that they're wrestling with? This is because they know that they are unlikely to receive the support and help at work that they need to handle the problem whilst performing their work tasks effectively.

If Arthur can support his colleague at a difficult time, being sure to understand his or her needs and priorities rather than just demanding that home life is kept at home, he will be doing a good job. Arthur realises the colleagues must meet their basic needs before they can concentrate on work.

## The Six Basic Human Needs

The famous American author and psychologist, Anthony Robbins - who has been a constant source of enlightenment for me throughout my life - took Maslow's hierarchy of needs and distilled the idea into his own list of six basic human needs:

### 1 Love and connection

This is a very important need for most people. If it is a high priority for you, you need to love, be loved and belong to teams at work or to groups of friends. You want to feel you are appreciated, accepted and involved.

## 2 Growth and learning

If you feel that growth is a particularly strong need, you want to learn continuously and experience lots of different things. Opportunities for personal growth are important to you.

## 3 Variety

Some give variety a very high priority in their lives. If this is you, you tend to get bored easily and need to be looking for the next interesting thing. You will have a wide variety of friends and hobbies to satisfy this need.

## 4 Significance and importance

This relates to Maslow's "esteem" in his hierarchy of needs. The feeling of significance comes in two parts: internal and external. Internal relates to satisfying yourself that you are doing something, which makes you feel important. External involves the image that you project to the outside world. If this is of particular significance, then you will be concerned with wearing the right clothes, driving the right car and having the right haircut so that people look at you, and you feel important.

## 5. Security

To satisfy the need for security in your life, you need to establish consistency and stability. There is also a need for law and order. Living free from worry is important to you if you give security high priority in your life.

## 6. Contribution

Contribution will be a high priority for you if you are the sort of person who likes to be doing things for others all the time. Examples of this would be helping out your family, working in a charity shop, and organising events for your local school or church. You will not be happy unless you are giving.

In order to understand why you make the decisions that you do, it is beneficial to look at the order of priority you put on your needs.

## Prioritising Your Needs

### Stalkie's Workout

*Take the list of six basic human needs. Beginning with just two of the needs, ask yourself which is more important. For example:*

*Question -  What is more important to me, 'love and connection' or 'growth'?*
*Your answer (for example): ' love and connection'*

*Now, ask yourself the next question by adding a further basic need to the one you chose as your first answer. To continue with our example:*

*Question - What is more important to me, 'love and connection' or 'variety'?'*

*Continue like this until you have gone through the whole list, using each need in turn.*

This is quite a complex process, so I have devised a table just like the one Arthur used (see right) to help you. By using this table, you will discover your number one need. If you continue this exercise with the remaining needs, again and again, you will have a final list of personal priorities. This list will help you to understand your own decision-making process.

Arthur's example of this exercise is filled in below; read it and then change it to your own needs.

| Question: Which is more important? | Answer: |
|---|---|
| **Part 1** | |
| Love and connection or growth | Love and connection |
| Love and connection or variety | Love and connection |
| Love and connection or significance | Love and connection |
| Love and connection or security | Love and connection |
| Love and connection or contribution | Love and connection |

From this we can see his number one need is love and connection - nothing is more important to him. In Part 2, Arthur continues with the exercise:

| **Part 2** | |
|---|---|
| Growth or variety | Growth |
| Growth or significance | Significance |
| Significance or security | Significance |
| Significance or contribution | Significance |
| Significance or growth | Significance |

So, Arthur went back to growth, to double-check, and it was confirmed as his number two need. He continues:

| **Part 3** | |
|---|---|
| Growth or variety | Growth |
| Growth or security | Security |
| Security or contribution | Security |
| Security or growth | Security |

Arthur's number three need turns out to be security.

| **Part 4** | |
|---|---|
| Significance or contribution | Contribution |
| Contribution or growth | Contribution |
| Contribution or variety | Contribution |

His number four need is contribution.

| **Part 5** | |
|---|---|
| Growth or variety | Growth |

This final part reveals the priority of Arthur's last two needs - his number five need is growth, and number six is variety.

After completing the exercise in this way, it was easy for Arthur to see that the order of priority for his six basic human needs was as follows:

- Love and connection
- Significance
- Security
- Contribution
- Growth
- Variety

How does this list compare to yours? And what can we deduce from it?

## Needs And Their Vehicles

> ***Raise Your Game Now!***
> *As we move on to explore your needs in more depth, I wish you to distinguish between a 'need' and a 'vehicle'. People often believe the vehicle is what they want but, in reality, it's the underlying need that the vehicle is supporting. A vehicle will supply you with a host of feelings, all of which directly feed your needs.*

A prime example of a vehicle is money. Money is not a need, it is not a value, it is a vehicle that you pay for things with - those things can then supply you with feelings that directly feed your needs. To illustrate; if you buy a car, it gives you the feeling of freedom, and freedom feeds the basic needs of security, significance and variety.

Likewise, I had a friend who was desperate to become a police officer, citing his need for 'job satisfaction'. In reality, the job proved to be the perfect vehicle to deliver his basic need for both external importance and for contribution.

"I'm giving you a vehicle that suits your needs, Thompson."

"Thanks. I'll have a Ferrari."

Looking at Arthur's list, the love and connection he gets from his family, friends and work colleagues is more critical to him than anything else – so, we can say that his vehicles for love and connection are the people around him. He achieves love and connection via his family, friends and colleagues.

However, Arthur's job is the next most important vehicle in his life; it provides him with a feeling of empowerment and importance, and it is this that feeds his need for significance. Arthur places more emphasis on this than security because he wouldn't mind changing his job, so long as he was moving to another significant position managing a store. That sort of move would give him more of a challenge, and his need for significance would be intensified by a bigger store – plus, he would presumably earn more money. This would again give him more significance and then, once he has overcome the initial challenge of variety (which he is not too keen on), Arthur would feel much more secure, especially since he would be earning more cash. He would find this increases the feeling of security that his job could give him.

Because Arthur gives significance quite a high priority, he likes to come home and let Mary know what he has achieved during the day. Naturally, Mary gives him all the praise that he craves for, and it makes him feel great. Mary has instinctively learnt to make her decisions on what she says to Arthur based on his needs. When Arthur discusses with Mary about the six basic human needs, she better understands why Arthur says and does certain things. Mary often makes a decision based on Arthur's need for importance and significance - she will not decide where to eat, what clothes to buy, or where to go on holiday without consulting him. This makes him feel important and significant, and she knows this. However, Arthur doesn't take Mary's needs into account when booking a holiday, for example, even though she obviously feels the need to contribute.

Although his need for significance is greater than that for security, Arthur does want to feel secure over and above his desire to contribute. But, his contribution to both work and home life are far more important to Arthur than his desire for growth and variety. He's not that bothered about learning new skills; he likes his routine. Going away to different places on holiday, meeting new friends and having new and varied experiences are not high on Arthur's wish list.

These things are not fixed in our lives though. After attending the Raise Your Game Now! seminar, Arthur could better see the benefits of growth and learning; he's now enjoying a better relationship with Mary and Kate as a direct result of what he learned. In addition, Arthur is now more likely to recognise growth and learning as being a really effective vehicle for improving his number one need – love and connection.

When Mary did the test she found that security, rather than significance, finished high on her list of priorities. Mary likes Arthur to make all the decisions for her; that way, she feels more secure. In this respect they are a great partnership, because the actions they naturally perform meet each other's needs.

## How to Identify and Meet Your Personal Needs

In a minute, I will be asking you to fill in a chart which will help you to realise where your needs are being met, or not met, in your life. It highlights your basic human needs and some of the vehicles that can help deliver them. The chart is just like a balance sheet in business which gives you a snapshot of where the business is at; it shows the assets and liabilities, and concludes whether the business is in profit or making a loss. Through your chart, you'll be able to see where you're at, which areas are important to you, and which are not working for you - your own assets and liabilities. You can then be the judge of whether you are in profit or in loss.

To get you in the swing, have a look at a chart that was filled in by someone that I recently coached - we'll call him 'Kit':

| Vehicles ▶ | Work | Wife | Children | Walking | Gardening |
|---|---|---|---|---|---|
| ▼ Needs | | | | | |
| Security | 8/10 | 7/10 | 9/10 | 9/10 | 9/10 |
| Variety | 9/10 | 4/10 | 10/10 | 10/10 | 9/10 |
| Significance | 10/10 | 4/10 | 10/10 | 8/10 | 7/10 |
| Love & Connection | 9/10 | 3/10 | 10/10 | 8/10 | 7/10 |
| Growth | 10/10 | 2/10 | 9/10 | 7/10 | 8/10 |
| Contribution | 10/10 | 4/10 | 8/10 | 7/10 | 10/10 |
| Total | 56/60 | 24/60 | 56/60 | 49/60 | 50/60 |
| Example | 24/60 | 24/60 x 100/1 = 2400/60 = 40% | | | |

The chart above indicates where Kit's needs are being met and where they are not being met. As you can see, the vehicles of 'work', 'children', 'walking' and 'gardening' provide his top scores. But, if we look at his 'work' score compared to his 'wife' score, we can extract some key information about the balance of his needs: Just imagine if Kit comes home from work and needs love and connection, security and to feel important - with a relationship that is only 40% effective, the support will not be there when he needs it. Also, if something great happened in his working life such as a promotion, the first person that you would normally wish to share these successes with would be your partner - again, regrettably, he doesn't appear to have a strong enough relationship. Clearly, I felt that Kit had to work on his relationship - not just the receiving but also the giving aspect of it - in order to correct the imbalance featured in his chart.

## Stalkie's Workout

*Now try filling in one of these charts for yourself and remember all your scoring must be true and honest. You will see that the blank chart lists all of the basic human needs in the first column and some examples of vehicles in the top column across – you can, of course, add your own vehicles to suit your life and interests.*

You will be no doubt tempted to put 'money' as one of your chosen vehicles... but, a word of caution here; money is never guaranteed to fulfil your dreams. Yes, it can certainly help, but I have coached people with many millions to their name and I can tell you that there is no direct link between wealth, an abundance of material things, and happiness. Your mind and body control your emotions - this is where true wealth resides.

Work through each human need, giving each of the primary vehicles in your life a score out of ten – ten means that the vehicle fulfils the need and one means that the vehicle does not fulfil that need. For example, if your children give you quite a lot of security then perhaps put a score of eight, and if they provide lots of variety in your life then maybe give that a nine and so on. Once you have given a mark for each need across all your vehicles, total the scores for each vehicle to discover just how effective they are being for you.

| Vehicles ▸ | Friends | Work |
|---|---|---|
| ▾ Needs | | |
| Security | | |
| Variety | | |
| Significance | | |
| Love & Connection | | |
| Growth | | |
| Contribution | | |
| Total | | |

By finding out exactly where your needs are being met and not being met, you will not only understand yourself better but you will also be in a position to start working on bringing a better balance to your life.

## Balancing Your Needs

At this time, we are going to focus upon the benefits of balancing your needs and how this can be achieved by interpreting your chart. To help us achieve this, I am going to use some case studies as a powerful way of illustrating how reading other people's charts can be used to help you read your own.

I recently coached three ladies who are all in business. They are all very high-powered women, with senior positions in either public or private companies. One is a Managing Director, one is a Marketing Director and one is an Operations Director. They control millions of pounds worth of budgets and hundreds, if not thousands, of people. Of course, they are all very well paid and respected within their organisations.

This is how their charts look:

## Managing Director

| Vehicles ▶ | Work | Friends | Child | Family | Partner |
|---|---|---|---|---|---|
| ▾ Needs | | | | | |
| Security | 10/10 | 10/10 | 9/10 | 5/10 | 5/10 |
| Variety | 10/10 | 10/10 | 10/10 | 5/10 | 5/10 |
| Significance | 10/10 | 5/10 | 9/10 | 4/10 | 5/10 |
| Love & Connection | 10/10 | 10/10 | 10/10 | 3/10 | 5/10 |
| Growth | 10/10 | 7/10 | 10/10 | 3/10 | 4/10 |
| Contribution | 10/10 | 9/10 | 10/10 | 6/10 | 3/10 |
| Total | 60/60 | 51/60 | 57/60 | 26/60 | 27/60 |

## Marketing Director

| Vehicles ▶ | Work | Friends | Home |
|---|---|---|---|
| ▾ Needs | | | |
| Security | 10/10 | 6/10 | 9/10 |
| Variety | 9/10 | 7/10 | 8/10 |
| Significance | 9/10 | 6/10 | 9/10 |
| Love & Connection | 10/10 | 5/10 | 6/10 |
| Growth | 10/10 | 4/10 | 6/10 |
| Contribution | 10/10 | 4/10 | 8/10 |
| Total | 57/60 | 32/60 | 46/60 |

## Operations Director

| Vehicles ▸ | Work | Daughter | Family | Dancing |
|---|---|---|---|---|
| ▾ Needs | | | | |
| Security | 8/10 | 8/10 | 8/10 | 5/10 |
| Variety | 10/10 | 10/10 | 7/10 | 9/10 |
| Significance | 10/10 | 10/10 | 6/10 | 5/10 |
| Love & Connection | 10/10 | 10/10 | 8/10 | 9/10 |
| Growth | 10/10 | 10/10 | 6/10 | 9/10 |
| Contribution | 10/10 | 10/10 | 6/10 | 5/10 |
| Total | 58/60 | 58/60 | 41/60 | 42/60 |

None of these women are in a successful relationship – two of the three have children but all are single at the moment. As you can see from their charts, all of them have major needs met at work and this has many repercussions in their lives. It particularly affects the balance of their lives and their significant relationships.

The two ladies who do have children have ended up using them to get their needs met. This isn't necessarily a bad thing – children can supply many of their parent's needs and will, of course, have many needs met by their parents in return. However, this should be seen in conjunction with all the other information in the chart. When needs are being met mainly or wholly by the children, most children will find this a burden.

This type of scenario is echoed in the movie, 'About a Boy' where a child lives alone with his mother. He is the centre of her life and vice versa, so he ends up doing anything to show his love for his mother. Scared to face reality, to look in the mirror and to appreciate that she does need to let go, the mother finds it difficult to accept that she has challenges and faults that need to be fixed – and quickly. She has forced her needs upon the boy. Her attitude is 'all men are bastards and I can cope without them, thank you very much', but the truth of the matter is that she is not coping alone. The relationship she has with her child is a substitute for the relationship she desires with a man. Rather than find the courage to develop a worthwhile relationship with a man, she finds it easier to satisfy her needs by putting pressure on her son.

These charts should help you realise that creating the correct balance in your life can impact positively upon others, but getting to this position requires an honest analysisof yourself. If you ever drift between relationship to relationship or job to job, there is no excuse for wondering why. If you tend to blame the other person, your employers, your upbringing, even your astrological chart, then perhaps you need to face up to your own weaknesses.

One of my ambitions in writing this book is to give every reader the power to look at themselves in an objective way, to discover the real person inside. This involves careful use of the techniques that I have been showing you and may sometimes be difficult or painful - but I guarantee that it will be worthwhile. If you do it honestly and conscientiously, you will improve and increase your talents. You will identify both your weak and positive areas. You will become a better person and will be able to live and care as an individual. This does not just benefit you, but it will also enable you to become an inspiration and role model for others. You will be able to use your authority and positively affect people within your circle of influence.

## Conflicts And Understanding The Needs of Others

Conflicts can surface in all sorts of circumstances, in the home, workplace, or in your social life. In these situations, if you have an understanding of how people's needs affect their behaviour, you will be able to diagnose why that conflict has arisen and act accordingly in the future.

Arthur's Area Manager, Darren, runs ten stores. Darren is under a lot of pressure from the organisation to meet targets and deadlines. Because of his status and position, Darren feels as though he is much more important than his store managers (even though in reality he is not more important - the people on the shop floor are the ones who put the money in the tills). When Darren goes into Arthur's store, the first thing he demonstrates is how much more important than Arthur he is. Darren highlights anything he can find that is incorrect. He often finds a poster that is hung in the wrong place, or he comments on the cleanliness of the store and remarks how some members of staff are inappropriately dressed. By pointing out all of these negative things, Darren is making himself feel more important. He also believes that he is contributing (negatively, as it turns out) to the running of the store. Darren is meeting five of his six basic human needs here; his significance, contribution, variety, security and connection.

Darren may tell himself that he really knows how to run a store - unlike these young lads today. He believes he has connected well with Arthur though, and really helped him along. Arthur, on the other hand, sees the situation in a very different way. Following the seminar, Arthur now understands why Darren acts like this; he used to think that Darren never really liked him, and wished he never had to endure a visit. It was a recipe for conflict.

The whole experience of Darren's visits used to make Arthur feel disillusioned, and provoked him to fight back. In response to his boss, Arthur refused to work late to get a job done, and didn't really care about his store's targets. The ripple effect of Darren's behaviour was immense. Arthur sought reassurance for his feelings about the Area Manager; as you can imagine, he was not very complimentary about Darren. He would take his frustration out on his colleagues, who also worked hard. Arthur met his needs by talking negatively to his colleagues about the Area Manager. This made him feel important, and gave him connection too. The trouble in this situation was that both men were meeting their needs negatively. Of course, Arthur's company would lose on all three accounts: Darren was de-motivating Arthur, Arthur was de-motivating his colleagues, and the company sales and morale were falling – and all so they could both meet their personal needs.

This can also happen in families too. If both parents want their needs to be met, an easy way to do it is through having an argument; both will tear the other person down, because they want to feel better by taking the power back. But who loses? The family, of course. Let's remember that, like a company, parents are both on the same team, so meeting needs negatively benefits nobody. This also occurred, you may recall, earlier in the book when Arthur complained about Mary not having supper ready on time.

> **Raise Your Game Now!**
> *You can either meet your needs with a 'positive act', or a 'negative act'. Let's look at a negative and then a positive way in which needs can be met:*

## A Negative Act

Through tearing down Arthur and his store, Darren is really being a terrorist by destroying what his colleague is trying to do. He liberally spreads fear, knowing he can make Arthur's life hard for him. Darren is wielding his power just to make himself feel better; he knows that whatever he says, Arthur can't come back at him because he will risk persecution. This is often a learned behaviour in both companies and families – for example, a boss may treat his employee in a certain way because that's how his parents behaved towards him when he was a child.

## The Positive Way

If Darren had been practising positive thoughts, along the lines of those discussed in the last chapter, then he would have gone into the store and found all the things that Arthur had done right, and then praised him for them. Darren would need to have belief in his own ability, and a good feeling of security, in order to do that. As a result, Arthur would be happy to see Darren during his visits, because he would associate his boss with praise; he would also emulate Darren's behaviour when dealing with his colleagues. If there were a few problems, Darren could say: "Arthur, your store is so great. Is there anything you would do to make it better?" of course, Arthur would be excited to try and think of things, making this a productive approach. Then, Darren could ask Arthur's permission: "If I see anything that could help, do you mind if I point it out?"

In this situation, Darren would have met his contribution, growth and learning, love and connection and security needs. More importantly, he would be raising his game and becoming a bright light, a solution to problems, and a true leader.

It is vital that you follow this example when dealing with family relationships. Go home and catch your husband or kids doing things right – then, ask them if they know how they can make it even better. Having learned this for himself, Arthur doesn't criticise Mary about dinner; he always finds two or three good points instead.

## Stalkie's Workout

*How do you think Darren and Arthur could behave in such a way that both their needs are fulfilled positively, whilst still getting the job done? Their aim of course is to make the store better, which in turn will sell more products. Choose the best approach that Darren could take in each of these two examples:*

**1 Darren should go into the store and:**

    **a** Praise all the good things he sees, and then ask, "What do you think needs to happen in your store in order to make it function more efficiently?"

    **b** Tell the staff: "That poster's crooked, there's some dust on the shelves, and some of your products are in the wrong place"

    **c** Tell the manager: "I could run this store much better – you'll never make Area Manager at this rate, Arthur."

**2 Darren should enter the store and declare:**

  **a** "You are doing a great job Arthur; your sales are increasing steadily – what do you think you could do to help sell even more?"

  **b** "Your staff are useless, and they don't look very good either – what are you going to do about it?"

  **c** "If you don't meet your targets next month then we are going to have to look at your future in the company."

Of course, by choosing '**a**' in both instances, Darren would be feeding Arthur's love and connection, significance, security, contribution, growth and learning needs whilst achieving the desired result, i.e. focussing on what is required of Arthur to make the store better. At the same time, he is reminding Arthur that he is in charge and doing a good job!

When a new colleague, Matt, joined Arthur's store it soon became apparent that he wanted to tear down the Manager, and the success he had made of the store. Very soon after Matt started work, he became highly successful at getting some of his colleagues to work against Arthur's directives. Matt was good looking, 'cool' and something of a 'Jack the lad'; his impressionable colleagues wanted to be a part of Matt's apparently cool lifestyle.

A disruptive person, like Matt, really needs to feel significant or important - he is termed a 'significance hunter'. But, he is gaining significance in a negative way, i.e. by creating his own little gang who want to get in the way of positive things – in this case, Arthur making a success of his store. When faced with this type of disruptive behaviour, there is a decision to make. Do you treat the person as a child and reprimand them, as Arthur would have in the past? Or, do you try to use your knowledge of their needs to respond to them in a more constructive fashion? Once upon a time, Arthur would have dealt with Matt by giving him discipline, but he learnt a new way of dealing with a disruptive colleague at the seminar and decided to give it a go.

First, Arthur tried a pattern interrupt. He called Matt into his office and told him that he was very impressed with his leadership skills. "Matt," he said, "you have managed to turn the whole store against my new ideas. Very well done. It took good communication skills, belief in your own ability, courage and determination. You really are doing well." Matt did not expect this - in fact, he was flabbergasted. Arthur also said, "Look Matt, you know you are very bright but, by destroying the profits of the shop, one of two things will happen; either we will have to let you go, or the company will close the shop, whereupon all your efforts will have simply had a negative effect on both you and me. How about using your skills positively?"

Arthur then suggested giving Matt a new role in the store - one that Arthur made sound very significant. He put Matt in charge of ensuring that customers were looked after in every way possible. Matt had to make sure that his colleagues greeted customers as soon as they walked in the door; that they weren't left standing confused looking at a product; that they knew where in the shop they could find what they were looking for. Arthur gave him a badge with 'Customer Liaison Manager' on it.

Matt was initially shocked by Arthur's proposal, but soon enough he was wearing his badge with pride and making sure he hit all his customer liaison targets. Through his tactics, Arthur had made sure that Matt could meet his significance need in a far more positive way. Now, he uses his skills as 'gang leader' to motivate his colleagues in a positive way, helping to ensure the shop runs smoothly and successfully as far as the customers are concerned.

### Raise Your Game Now!
*You can turn a potential 'terrorist' in your life into one of your biggest supporters simply by understanding their basic human needs.*

The same applies to all spheres of your life. When James, the youngest child in the Collins family, has the desire to feel important just like his dad, Mary tries to satisfy his need. She gives him a 'special' role in the house, and says things like "only grown-ups are allowed to put DVD's in the machine - do you think you would be careful enough?" and "mummies are in charge of tidying up - do you think you know where everything goes?" By doing this, she is empowering him - albeit supervised - and his need for importance is met. Mary could take this further by telling James that he is in charge of the DVD's, and that it's his job to make sure they are all put away. This is using James' need for importance in a constructive, rather than destructive, way.

### Raise Your Game Now!

*All of your basic human needs are ever-present, sitting in your sub-conscious mind and just below the surface. You are not usually consciously aware of them, but they're definitely there, lurking behind every decision that you make.*

When you begin to successfully understand the needs of both yourself and others, you will realise what it is that you should change about your behaviour to ensure you get the very best possible outcome from every situation. You will become aware of what makes others feel good, and what motivates them. Then, you will be able to play to their needs and achieve your own outcome.

# The Fourth Round
## *Enjoying Yourself*
### 13 Praise Your Game Now!

**Arthur has discovered that gratitude, having the right attitude and becoming responsible for his own actions are all interdependent. What's more, they work in harmony to create strong beliefs. The more gratitude Arthur has, the better attitude he seems to adopt and the more control he has over his life. Moreover, he now has a strong self-belief in what he is able to achieve. It is hard to comprehend that Arthur was once a very negative person who never celebrated his colleagues' successes; now, he makes a point of finding a way to celebrate anything good or positive that happens each day. Praising and celebrating an individual's strengths and success levels, however small they may be, is something that falls into the arena of positive psychology.**

In the years immediately following the Second World War, psychology was a science largely devoted to healing - it concentrated on repairing damage. This neglected the idea of a fulfilled individual. Now, psychological treatment is not just about fixing what is wrong; it's also about building things that are right. The aim of positive psychology is to move on from repairing the worst things in life to building the best qualities in life. Positive psychology aims to measure, understand and then build human strengths and virtues.

# Build on Your Strengths

When Arthur first became the manager of his store, he used all the knowledge he'd gained through working for other companies to help him in the job. Arthur really enjoyed his role, and thought his management was second to none; as he witnessed his colleagues making sales, he gave himself a pat on the back. He was doing what he loved to do, and he just wanted to become better and better. After a while, Arthur noticed how some of his colleagues were good at closing deals, and others were better at creating a rapport with customers; armed with this information, he decided to work on each of his colleagues' weaknesses.

Arthur put those who were good at closing deals in charge of greeting customers as they entered the store, whereupon they could build a rapport with them. Meanwhile, he put those who were great at first impressions and building a rapport with customers in charge of closing deals. Arthur believed he was being an excellent manager; his plan to work on his colleagues' weaknesses, Arthur thought, was very smart.

To begin with, the staff accepted Arthur's decision, and tried very hard in their new roles. However, it was not long before they started to become frustrated at their inability to succeed, whereupon they all wanted to get back to what they were good at. Despite the obvious downturn of his store's fortunes, Arthur persisted with the programme; he was convinced that, by working on his colleagues' weaknesses, he would be able to produce a workforce that would be strong in all areas.

After a month on the programme, the team's morale really began to drop. As Arthur pushed his colleagues further and further, they felt ever more humiliated; in truth, Arthur's programme had only succeeded in confirming what his staff's weaknesses were. The colleagues expressed their concerns to Arthur, but no matter what they said, or how the figures read, Arthur would not budge. He firmly believed this was the way to great success.

However, everything changed when Arthur attended a motivational seminar; finally, he began to realise that his attempts at improving people's weaknesses constituted a very negative form of training. Instead, Arthur should have been focusing on building his colleagues' strengths. The workforce already had talent and enthusiasm for their jobs, and all Arthur needed to do was highlight those assets. Through encouraging their strengths and rewarding success, Arthur could ensure that his colleagues would work as a team, and excel. The staff would be doing what they enjoyed, and were good at; as a by-product, the store would become more profitable.

A commonly held belief is that we can fix things which are wrong by focusing on weaknesses. In this book, we've seen examples of this not only in the early approaches to psychology, discussed at the beginning of the chapter, but also in Arthur's actions. Moreover, there are parallels with the way in which I was treated at school. My strengths were ignored, my weaknesses worked on and the result was 'no real improvement'. It is plain to see that this view is not productive, and if we want to succeed, we must take a positive approach through building on our strengths.

## Do What You Love, Love What You Do

Your personal strengths are the things you are good at. When you use your strengths, they tend to produce feelings of pride and satisfaction; a strength can be anything, including artistic talents, selling, gardening etc. These become strengths when you devote a significant amount of time to them and, as you do so, your feelings of pride and satisfaction grow.

Think back to what you really enjoyed doing at school. Was it English, maths, cookery or sport? Science, perhaps? Whatever subject you enjoyed, you were most probably good at it. Through taking part in that activity and succeeding, you would have experienced a feeling of satisfaction coming over you. Rachel, the youngest Collins family daughter, remembers watching the Olympics as a little girl; she used to think the swimmers looked fabulous as they glided through the water, and she dreamt about how nice it would be to do that herself one day.

Rachel yearned to swim like the Olympians on television. Your own yearnings act rather like a magnetic pull, guiding you towards one thing rather than another. In Rachel's case, she found herself being pulled towards the world of sport; when she was very young, her desire was especially strong. Our earliest yearnings to do something or be someone are very powerful, and this can be the start of something great. However, yearning for something does not stop when you become an adult, indeed you may have a really strong desire to start your own business for example - these yearnings are also extremely powerful.

Mary identified, very early on, Rachel's desire to be involved with sports; as Rachel got older, Mary worried that the fame sport could bring was the only thing driving her daughter in this direction. However, as soon as Mary saw her daughter compete in, and win, her first swimming competition, she realised that sport really was Rachel's passion. Rachel was pleased to win, but wanted to improve herself in order to compete again. The win was a pleasant by-product of being involved in the competition itself. Seeing Rachel's satisfaction at being involved with the sport, Mary knew nothing would stop her from going to the top.

It must be said that satisfaction and competency are not always partners. Despite being the best in her class at school - she is brilliant academically - Rachel does not gain much satisfaction from this competency, and for that reason it is not a strength. On the other hand, when it comes to sport, Rachel has a real talent and it gives her a large amount of satisfaction when taking part. Sporty people can be divided into two categories: they can be naturals, or they can be 'competents'. Both types of people are fast learners in their field. However, competents learn through traditional methods such as textbooks, whereas naturals get there by just doing it. Rachel is a natural - she simply jumped in and gave it a go, learning in the process that she was good. By experiencing the swimming, she quickly learnt even more.

***Raise your Game!***
*A strength can be determined by the presence of rapid learning, and the continuation of that learning throughout a lifetime.*

## A Glimpse of Excellence

Positive psychology is all about knowing your strengths, using these effectively and then building on them. Rachel knows her strength is sport - swimming, to be specific. She recognises this through her desire to do it, her satisfaction when she is a part of it, and by spotting a moment of excellence in her performance. Rachel has an inner ability, and this is something that she can demonstrate with her swimming.

There is no doubt that Rachel wants to pursue her strength and build on her successes. Positive psychology is very important here; first of all, she needs to do more swimming, because practice will make perfect. In addition, Rachel must enjoy it, relive her successes and celebrate her triumphs. The more you think of yourself doing your very best work, the more you are encouraging success in the future. Use visualisation (look back at Kate's case study in the 'Believe in Yourself' chapter for an example of how to utilise this technique) to picture yourself winning over and over - try writing about it, and talking about it.

Through positively thinking about your strengths, you can create great things. If Rachel practices, visualises herself in the future and celebrates her successes, she will become what she wants to be, i.e. a great sportswoman.

# Discovering Your Strengths

## *Stalkie's Workout*

There are four ways in which you can discover your own strengths, just like Rachel. Try answering the following questions to see where your strengths lie:

### 1 Yearnings

What always interested you as a child? What did you really want to do? What sort of person did you want to become?

### 2 Satisfaction

What gives you satisfaction? What task, when you complete it, makes you feels good?

### 3 Rapid learning

What activity do you find you can pick up really easily? What do you do that keeps building on your accomplishments?

### 4 Glimpses of excellence

When do you see yourself doing something great? When does your performance of excellent quality occur?

# Using Your Strengths

Look at your answers; these are activities you love to do, aren't they? Think how you could incorporate one or more of these things into your life, if they aren't already. If you enjoy dancing, maybe you could do some work for a dance magazine, undertake some extra dance classes, or help out in a theatre with marketing - you could even volunteer to run a children's dance group. If you enjoy drawing and painting, take time out to do more. Maybe you should try interior design in your own home, or you could attend a painting club and help those who want to learn how to do it. There are many ways in which you can incorporate the things you love to do into your life. By doing this, you will be building on - and using - your strengths.

## Recognising Weaknesses

I should say from the outset that weaknesses are not everything you don't do well - a weakness is only such when it intrudes on areas that you are great at, thereby lessening your confidence. When you find a weakness, it is important to manage it, and not to think that it can be turned into a strength. Weaknesses can be removed, reduced or corrected with a large amount of time, energy and in some cases money but they cannot be transformed into strengths.

Attempting to convert weaknesses to strengths wastes time. Cast your mind back to Arthur's plan for improving his colleagues; it failed because he was focusing on weaknesses. The aim, therefore, is to manage weaknesses so that strengths are free to develop without interruption. In this way, the strengths will become even stronger and the weaknesses are relegated to the status of being irrelevant.

Before Arthur attended his motivational seminar, he was very stressed by his job. As the manager of a large retail store, he had lots of responsibilities. Arthur's wife Mary - who works part time at the local school, when she's not looking after the family home and their three children - always tries to show Arthur how appreciative she is of all his hard work. On one occasion, Mary cooked a special meal for Arthur consisting of his favourite sausage, mashed potato and vegetables; the children were occupied elsewhere. When Arthur got home, the dinner was on the table so the couple sat down for their evening meal.

As he took his seat, Arthur said "the football is on tonight, so why didn't you save dinner until later? I wanted to watch the match - why didn't you check with me to see when I wanted to eat?" Mary had spent a lot of time, energy and effort preparing the meal for her husband. She felt really disappointed and deflated because rather than appreciating her efforts, all Arthur could do was comment on the fact that the dinner had been served too early for him - she'd got it wrong.

Unfortunately, worse was to come. "And why haven't we got gravy?" said Arthur. This was too much for Mary - "You can cook your own dinner in future!" she said.

Arthur's old behaviour illustrates the complete opposite of positive psychology. Instead of catching Mary doing things right and praising her for them, he just commented on her weaknesses; this is very de-motivating.

With Arthur continually focusing on Mary's weaknesses, her strengths never got noticed. Unfortunately, we live in a culture where we tend to focus on weaknesses; our instinct is to identify them, and then to attempt a fix. Managing weaknesses rather than trying to put them right is a very challenging concept to understand and put into practice.

"But you know I wanted to see how Colchester Utd. would get on in the replay against Gravesend."

# Managing Weaknesses

Mary had always felt as though her home cooking was weak - she loves preparing food, but Mary could become very defensive when anyone mentioned the subject. She always said that if she had more time, she would be better at it. However, despite her defensive mentality, Mary almost obsessively tried to correct and build on her weakness by trying to cook difficult things. She prepared meals for her husband whenever possible.

Although Mary tried hard and spent many hours in the kitchen, she was very slow at learning the techniques required for cooking. She once booked herself onto a cookery class in the evenings; it didn't help a great deal, and despite the professional teachers encouraging her, Mary had little joy. Slow growth in this problem area led to Mary going through repetitive training, with little or no gain. Mary always thought that, if she could just hang in there, she would eventually be successful. By plodding away at her weakness, Mary's strengths were forgotten.

When practising her home cooking, Mary just wanted to get it over and done with. If you concentrate on doing something that you are not good at, it consumes you and leaves little energy for thoughts of the future. When occupying yourself with something you can and like to do, you obtain a vision of the future, and where your talents could lead you. Mary's weakness was her cooking; whenever she did it, she just wanted to be finished as quickly as possible before moving on to something else.

In your own life, you will have to recognise your weaknesses - they are not simply everything you don't do well, but rather the things which affect your performance, or lower your self-esteem. Having done this, you can set about finding ways of managing them. For example, if your writing skills give you cause for concern, try to lessen the importance of having that ability in your daily life. You could make reports easier to write by setting up templates, or pass each writing task on to an assistant who is more skilled than you. Ignore the instinctive feelings you have to try and fix your weaknesses; find ways of managing them instead.

> **Raise Your Game Now!**
> *Recognise weaknesses in yourself and manage them - don't waste your time trying to turn them into strengths.*

## Catch People Doing Things Right

When it came to Mary's cooking, Arthur always used to point out her weaknesses and did not pay attention to her strengths such as her thoughtfulness, organisational skills and persistence. By focusing on someone's weaknesses, you are focusing on negatives. Thinking positively is all about building the best things in life, i.e. your strengths.

Consider the following example: Jack and Hannah's twin boys are given unconditional love; Hannah will always catch them doing something right, even if it is really small. When they both started to walk, Hannah celebrated each small step as if there was no tomorrow. If they fell on their first attempt they were praised for such good effort, and not criticised for falling.

Jack and Hannah always focus on their sons' strengths and never on their weaknesses - they celebrate each good thing as much as they can. Unconditional love and encouragement is all that's required for success. Everyone wants their special achievements to be celebrated, and encouragement of this kind is very powerful and often overlooked in many areas of life, especially when it comes to business and education.

## Celebrate!

Arthur's brother Ryan had always smoked. No one else in the family smokes, and they always tried to discourage him from the habit. When he could endure his family's constant nagging no longer, Ryan made the decision to quit. He smoked 60 a day, so it was always going to be a tough journey; after many false starts, Ryan had his daily quota down to only ten. Despite his obvious success, he felt disappointed that he was still a smoker. His family, on the other hand, were very proud of Ryan, and Arthur in particular felt there was something to celebrate.

Ryan felt disappointed with himself; he only recognised his weakness, i.e. the fact that he could not give up completely. On the other hand, Arthur could see Ryan's powers of persistence, willingness and determination. By looking positively at the situation, Arthur felt Ryan's success was worth celebrating. Giving up 50 cigarettes a day, with only 10 more to go - why, that was going to save lots of money, perhaps enough for Ryan to buy next year's football season ticket! There are often many things to celebrate that will encourage further success.

Once Arthur had seen the error of his ways with Mary, he viewed all aspects of life differently - Mary's cooking, Rachel's swimming, Ryan's attempt to give up smoking, even Kate's weight loss. He began to catch them all doing things right, and made sure that he celebrated each and every occasion. They all had their strengths and victories, whether minor or major, recognised and celebrated.

## Praise your Game Now!

Whether you are trying to lose weight, become fit, stop smoking, save money or start a business etc. you need to catch yourself doing things right. You can even take the pluses out of making what may at first seem to be a mistake; view the error as a learning experience. Catching yourself doing things right is the fuel of self-perpetuation.

It is true that some great things are created in isolation, however the real magic happens when there is celebration for it.

# The Final Round
## *Your Game Plan*

### 14 Doing Life

#### Your Plan of Action!

**So this is it. The Game of Life. And we're all in it.**

Throughout the last 13 chapters, you have been introduced to the rules of the <u>**GAME**</u> - **G**ratitude and **A**ttitude, **M**aking a friend, and **E**njoying yourself. You have also explored the key tactics such as being healthy, facing fears, meeting needs, moving behaviour towards values, building on strengths, and many many more. An honest, meaningful understanding of these tactics will clearly help you to Raise Your Game Now!

Now you know the rules, now you know the tactics, I have designed this final chapter with a specific aim in mind - to create your own personal game plan which can start working for you within the few hours that it will take to complete it.

This plan of action will allow you to play the Game of Life like you've never played it before - to live every minute of it with feeling in your heart, to set new standards, to make an impact, to let people see your true colours.

**So remember; action supersedes everything. To read it and do nothing is to waste it.**

# Guidelines for Creating Your Plan

■ To fulfil your true potential, you must commit yourself to these guidelines. Your life is worth the investment.

■ Make sure you have plenty of time on your hands to complete the Stalkie Workouts. At least a whole morning, afternoon or evening would be good. This must not be rushed. You are planning your life.

■ Find somewhere calm and quiet where you can really think and where you won't be interrupted. Unplug your 'phone, turn your mobile and pager off and get a grip.

■ Make sure you complete all of the Workouts.

So, grab a pen and paper... good luck, have fun and keep your spirit high.

LIFE PLAN

Sit around on my fat arse doing nothing

Moan about the fact that it didn't change anything

# Becoming the Architect of Your Life

Have you ever planned your life? Maybe you have a daily, or even weekly, 'things to do' list. You've probably planned a holiday, a house move, maybe a wedding... but your life? I doubt it.

I want you to become the architect of your life. To take control of building it just the way you want it - to make you feel the most fulfilled and ultimately the happiest you can possibly be.

If you don't know what it is you want out of life then how can you achieve it? You wouldn't dream of getting on a train without knowing your destination; you wouldn't start to build a house without knowing how you wanted the finished product to look - you would have an architect's plan to help you on your way.

To lead a life that is truly second to none, you must become the architect of your life.

Let's start with an exercise that excites me everytime I witness it being done - and I've witnessed it being done literally thousands of times. Watching someone conceive a game plan for their life is a real buzz... I know how much pleasure you can create for yourself and for those around you by acting upon it. The more passion you put into the exercise, the better the blueprint for a new you will emerge.

## *Stalkie's Workout*

*Consider these points;*

*A Think about what makes you happy and the most fulfilled.*

*B Put these elements into the ultimate vision that you are striving for.*

*C Think about what tools you might need; what strategy you need to implement. Think about the blueprint you require to create your ultimate vision. Make some points now that you consider the most important to you.*

## Are you struggling with this?

It is my job, as your personal coach, to help you realise those elements that make you feel most happy and fulfilled; to find the tools that will help you devise a plan and a strategy to achieve them. In short, together we are going to plot your future game plan.

## Vision Making

You may believe that goal setting, or vision making (as I like to call it), is old-fashioned or a waste of time. You may think you've heard it all before. But, the truth is that people, cultures and societies – indeed the world – would not evolve unless somebody somewhere had a vision or goal in mind.

Eddison had the vision to produce artificial light; Ghandi had the vision to gain independence for India; Bill Gates had the vision to revolutionise communication via computers; David Beckham had the vision of being the best footballer in the world.

In every century, in every class, in every culture, in every society there is somebody with a vision. Somebody who wants to change and develop what is considered the norm. Somebody who wants to think and act outside the box.

### Stalkie's Workout

*Think about what you have already achieved in life, what goals you have already completed, what visions you have already accomplished. Take at least five minutes to do this – it may take you longer. This should be fun! See if these memories can evoke the emotions that you felt at the time.*

*Remember; you only get out of this Workout what you put in.*

# Are You an Achiever?

Your answer will relate to how you perceive yourself. The bigger your list above then the more likely you will answer yes to this question. However, some of you may struggle to even find a handful of answers.

Let us look at what you may have already achieved;

- You can walk
- You can talk
- You can run
- You can feed yourself
- You can ride a bicycle
- You can drive a car
- You have bought a house
- You have built relationships
- You can work
- You can earn money
- You have possessions
- You have clothes on your back
- You can love
- You can care for others

And so the list goes on. You see you have achieved many things in your lifetime already.

Now remember how you felt about these accomplishments. When a child says his or her first words they are jubilant, and the result is happy and strong praise from the parents or carer. When a child first walks, the happiness that they are experiencing is clearly evident and there is yet more praise. When you moved in to your first home – whether bought or rented – that feeling of independence was overwhelming. Remember that tingle of your first kiss?

I want you to experience those feelings all over again. That's what life is about.

**Taking this into consideration, how do you feel now?**
- You are an achiever!
- You should be smiling!

## Your Life: Five Component Parts

Try looking at your life divided into the following five component parts;

- **Health** - Your foundations
- **Self** - Pillar 1
- **Relationships** - Pillar 2
- **Finance** - Pillar 3
- **Possessions** - Pillar 4

Lets' continue using the analogy of building a house here. Of these five elements the most important component is HEALTH.

## Your Foundations

In The First Round, Getting Match Fit, we discussed how the quality of your health provides the foundations for the rest of your life. You will not flourish in any other area without vitality and a strong healthy body. If you wake up in the morning feeling bad then you will struggle at whatever area you are working on.

*Remember; you must nurture and maintain the vehicle that takes you through life – your body.*

# Your 4 Pillars

The remaining four components each form a pillar of the house we are going to build together.

## Pillar 1

**Self** – your personal identity or personality. This is what makes you unique. The self consists of your 'being' - your emotions, your spirituality, your values, needs, beliefs - all of which are developed by what you absorb from your 'doing', such as your education, socialisation and lifestyle.

## Pillar 2

**Relationships** – with friends, family, work colleagues, social circle or the members of your sports team.

## Pillar 3

**Finance** – this is the fuel in the majority of people's lives. Without money we are unable to do the things that are required of us. To feed, clothe and house ourselves; to build our assets; to provide a financial security. It is very challenging to live in this world without money.

## Pillar 4

**Possessions** – many people equate how happy they are and how successful they have become by their material possessions; what type of car they own, what size of house they live in, the clothes they wear.

# Giving Each Pillar Value

The value of each of these pillars differs from individual to individual. For example;

- Relationships – Person A is happy with just one or two close friends that can be relied upon. Those are the relationships that make person A most fulfilled and happy. In contrast, person B is happiest with lots of acquaintances and would never feel fulfilled with just one or two friends.

- Finance – Person A won't be content until they have become the Chief Executive Officer of ICI, however person B wants nothing more than a part time job.

The value of every person's pillars are different. Each individual will be happy with a different self-development, a different set of relationships, a different set of financial circumstances and different number of possessions.

But the foundations – health. Health should be of the same value to each and every person. Everybody should strive to be healthy and vibrant to work at their optimum.

## *Stalkie's Workout*

*Look at the five component parts of your life. What I would like you to do now is give each pillar a mark out of 10. How do you view that particular area of your life right now? Is it great and cannot be improved, or does it need to be worked on?*

*Give each part a mark out of 10 - and be honest with yourself: 1 being 'terrible', 'it couldn't be any worse' and 10 being 'the best'.*

|  | Your Mark |
|---|---|
| ■ Foundations: Health | ............ |
| ■ Pillar 1: Self | ............ |
| ■ Pillar 2: Relationships | ............ |
| ■ Pillar 3: Finance | ............ |
| ■ Pillar 4: Possessions | ............ |

What are your scores??

If your health has scored less than 10 then we have room for improvement. Why? Because the foundations of your house are already a little shaky.

Now lets look at each of the pillars. Perhaps three of your pillars have scored well and you have given them a mark of 6 or 7, but the third one has scored low, perhaps a 2 or a 3. When you come to put the roof on what happens? The roof is unbalanced and it comes tumbling down.

What you are trying to achieve is a balance and harmony between all four of the pillars so that the roof stays put! You also want to feel happy in each of these areas – you want a score as near to 10 as is humanly possible. That way you will build a beautifully proportioned house to keep you happy, safe and secure...

If you have scored below a 10 in any of the five areas then I would like us to work on them together - to build an ultimate vision. To decide what it is that would make you happier and more fulfilled.

## The Five Ws

1 **WHAT** is your vision or goal, the outcome you desire?

2 **WHY** do you want/desire this vision? This is really important. You must have a compelling reason to want to achieve your vision.

3 **WHAT** action(s) are you going to take to achieve your vision?

4 **WHAT** are you going to use to achieve this vision? What resources are you going to enlist to help you in your actions to achieve your goal?

5 **WHEN** are you going to achieve your vision by – when is your deadline?

'Doing Life' is about creating a game plan based upon your life vision and then making it happen! This we will achieve together by applying 'the 5 W's' to your foundations and then, in turn, to each of your pillars.

# Creating Your Life Vision

## Vision 1 - Your Foundations

Let's now analyse your foundations – your health. To help you formulate your vision I will use the example of Sandy, a special client of mine:

**1** <u>Sandy, what is your health vision?</u>

I would like to be slimmer and I'd like to lose at least a stone in weight.

**2** <u>Why do you want to be lighter or slimmer?</u>

I feel a general lack of self-confidence; I know I'm not healthy and I feel very down about myself.

<u>How does that lack of self-confidence make you feel?</u>

It makes me feel horrid – absolutely rotten.

<u>So feeling bad about yourself has given you low self-esteem?</u>

Absolutely right.

**3** <u>What are you going to do to change the situation?</u>

To lose the weight I'm going to join a slimming club, join a gym and start looking a bit closer at the food I'm eating.

**4** <u>What resources and support are you going to use?</u>

I'm going to find a friend who wants to lose weight, too, I know plenty of them, so that we can work together.

I'm not going on a faddy diet – I'm going to make an effort to understand a bit more about food, what it does to the body. My friend knows a nutritionalist and I'm going to make an appointment with them.

**5** <u>When are you going to do this by?</u>

I want to lose a stone in year as I think this is achievable and is a more healthy way of losing weight rather than the crash dieting as I have done before. But my friend and I are meeting up next week to start making plans!!

*Now you make your notes. Answer the questions below. You may have more than one health goal, in which case write them all down:*

■ Is it to lose weight?
■ To find a solution to a niggling health problem?
■ To exercise more?
■ Are you tired all the time?
■ Do you have a headache?
■ Lots of colds?
■ Too many days off sick?
■ Lack of vitality?

Please remember that the bigger the vision; the more compelling the reason; the clearer the actions; the stronger the resources - the more likely you are to achieve this goal.

## *Stalkie's Vision 1 Workout*

*1 What is your health vision?*

*2 Why do you want to achieve this/these vision(s)?*

*3 What are you going to do to build towards your vision(s)?*

*4 What resources and support are you going to use?*

*5 When are you going to do this/these by?*

## Vision 2 - Your Self

Let's analyse Pillar 1 – your 'self'. To help you formulate your self vision, let's take a look at what David, who attended one of my seminars, wants for his 'self'. David has recently undergone a life-saving operation so his perspective on life has changed recently.

**1** <u>David, what is your vision of your 'self'?</u>

When I finally go to my grave I want to be seen as a caring, thoughtful and intelligent person. Somebody who really cared for others...

**2** <u>Why do you want that?</u>

Having been through a life-changing experience I have come to realise what is important to me... and what is important to me is helping people who are less fortunate than myself.

**3** <u>What are you going to do about it?</u>

I have very few skills that I can use to help people. I am not a qualified doctor, or nurse. But I can help those who are less fortunate than myself by being an 'ear'; lending a hand; just being there.

**4** <u>What are you going to use?</u>

I am going to start by going to my local church and finding out ways in which I can help in the community. Hopefully they are going to point me in the right direction. I will also contact local charities to see what they need doing.

**5** <u>When are you going to achieve this goal?</u>

I think this goal is ongoing. I don't think you can ever be caring, or thoughtful enough. It's a growing process. But I will start to make a change in my life tomorrow. I will be helping out somewhere next week and I want to have made a difference to someone's life a year from now...

*Look at your 'self'. What is it you want to improve upon? What emotions and needs do you want to feed?*

- What is your vision?
- Do you want to become more cultural?
- Visit the theatre more often?
- Take in an art gallery or two?
- Do you want to become more travelled?
- Visit other lands?
- Experience other cultures?
- Do you want to start understanding the meaning of life?
- Understand religion?
- Play a musical instrument?
- Learn a language?
- Play a new sport?
- Become more caring?
- Do volunteer work?
- Start to teach?
- Learn a martial art?
- Become a singer?
- Record an album?
- Be the next Christmas No.1?

## Stalkie's Vision 2 Workout

*1 What is/are your vision(s) of your 'self'?*

*2 Why do you want to achieve this/these vision(s)?*

*3 What are you going to do to build towards your vision(s)?*

*4 What resources and support are you going to use?*

*5 When are you going to complete this vision by?*

## Vision 3 – Relationships

Let's analyse Pillar 2 – relationships. To help us take a look at how you view your relationships, I have spoken to Emily who is a 45-year-old mother of two.

**1** <u>Emily, what is your vision vis-à-vis your relationships?</u>

I want a happy and fulfilling relationship with my partner of 25 years.

**2** <u>Why do you want this?</u>

Because we have been growing apart recently and the relationship isn't good at the moment but I don't want to throw away 25 years of being together. I believe it is worth working at...

**3** <u>What are you going to do about it?</u>

I'm going to make more time for him, talk to him and confide in him. I want to tell him how I feel and what I want in the hope that he feels the same way. I'm going to suggest we seek some outside help.

**4** <u>What are you going to use?</u>

I'm going to seek out a counsellor via friends that I know who have been through the same problem. I'm going to use my time more effectively in relation to him ie spend more time together.

**5** <u>When are you going to do this by?</u>

I'm going to start immediately but I'd like to see some positive results in six months time. I'm realistic enough to know that I won't see results immediately.

*Now, how do you feel in the context of your relationships?*

- Do you feel you could have a better relationship with your wife or partner?
- Could you relate to your children more?
- Would you like to have more friends?
- Do you want your colleagues at work to like you more?
- Are you guilty of blaming others for your relationship problems?
- Do you have trouble meeting new people?
- Do you need to listen more?
- Show more compassion to your loved ones?
- Do you need to love the things your kids love?
- Are you grumpy when you should be loving in your relationships?

**Remember; this is life. There is no time out. We want to make your day the best it can possibly be because you are never going to have this day again.**

## Stalkie's Vision 3 Workout

**Sit up and take a deep breath – you are building your future NOW!**

*1 What is/are your relationship/s vision(s)?*
*2 Why do you want to achieve this/these vision(s)?*
*3 What are you going to do to build towards your vision(s)? The action.*
*4 What resources and support are you going to use?*
*5 When are you going to complete this/these vision(s) by?*

## Vision 4 – Finance

Now we're moving on to your finance Pillar. I've asked Ben to help us work on this one together. Ben has given himself a score of just 3 on his finance pillar.

**1** <u>Ben, what is your finance vision? What do you hope to achieve here for yourself?</u>

I'm self-employed and I really want to open my own studio and be my own boss.

**2** <u>Why is it that you want to do this?</u>

I want to be involved in the music industry. I love making music and want the freedom of being my own boss and doing my own work.

<u>What about the freedom, Ben?</u>

Well, I'm a music producer. I want to make my own choices as to the bands I am going to produce.

**3** <u>What action are you going to take to achieve this?</u>

I've just got involved with a promoter and we're going to open a small studio and promote the acts that we produce there.

<u>How are you going to develop it?</u>

We've drawn up a business plan and we're looking at grant funding and other ways in which we can start up. We also need to form relationships with bands and other music industry people.

**4** <u>What resources are you going to use?</u>

We've got most of the equipment we need and friends in the industry who can help out.

**5** <u>When are you planning on doing this by?</u>

We have a five month business plan so the wheels are in motion.


*Over to you. Really think about this. Finance is the fuel that powers a lot of your life.*

■ Where do you want to work?

■ How much money do you want to earn?

■ What assets do you want to build?

■ What will make you happy?

■ Are you using your money beneficially?

■ Could you earn more money?

■ Are you really fulfilling your potential?

■ How high is high?

---

## *Stalkie's Vision 4 Workout*

*1 What is/are your finance vision/s?*

*2 Why do you want to achieve this/these vision/s?*

*3 What are you going to do to build towards your vision/s?*

*4 What resources and support are you going to use?*

*5 When are you going to complete this vision by?*

---

## Vision 5 – Possessions

Take a look at the people you know. Some place a lot of value on possessions – they strive for designer labels, flash cars, big houses – and there are others who have very little requirement for such things. You must think about what will make you happy.

Here's what Bob has to say about his own possession vision. Bob is a characterful, 28-year-old entrepreneur.

**1** <u>Bob, what possessions do you visualise owning?</u>

I want a big detached house; I want to drive a Ferrari; I want to dress in the very latest designer clothing. I want all the good things that money can buy.

**2** <u>Why do you place so much value on these possessions?</u>

My clothes and the car I drive make me feel good. People will stop and look at the car – admire it, aspire to it and I want to be the one who has it. It's a way of measuring my success.

**3** <u>What are you going to do to achieve those things?</u>

I'm going to work hard. I'm going to knuckle down and network and further my career.

**4** <u>What are you going to use, what resources, to elevate you to this position?</u>

I'm going to use the contacts I've got now. The relationships I've made in the past have got me to where I am now. I've not got a Ferrari but I've got a nice car. I'm going to keep doing what I'm doing – but more of it and get better at it.

**5** <u>When are you going to achieve your final vision?</u>

I want to have it all by the time I am forty... Money in the bank and I want to settle down in a nice house.

*Now it's your turn again. Think of yourself as a child at Christmas – list everything you really want; a car; a villa abroad; jewellery; a stunning garden; a cottage in the country... Start writing your list now... an apartment in Paris, beach house in Hawaii, racing cars, planes, boats, scuba diving equipment, football pitch in your own garden, own beauty salon, your own hairdresser, own a health farm, swimming pool, golf course, steam room, gym?*

## Stalkie's Vision 5 Workout

**1** *What possessions do you want?*

**2** *Why do you want to own these possessions?*

**3** *What are you going to do to get them?*

**4** *What resources and support are you going to use?*

**5** *When are you going to get them by?*

Hopefully I have triggered your thought processes and helped you identify the areas that need to be worked upon.

Remember we are trying to create a life for you that is fulfilling for you – one that makes you truly happy...

# Formulating Your Game Plan

I hope you completed the Workouts as honestly and as thoroughly as possible because now is the crunch time - if you haven't, go back and start again. There is no point in proceeding if you haven't done the Workouts or been true to yourself.

## Stage 1

Now you must write all your visions on a chart* that quite clearly depicts the 5 Ws – What? Why? What? What? and When? – culminating with the deadline.

*You can download charts from www.stalkie.com and www.raiseyourgamenow.com

You will see from the examples that I have given that deadlines differ between people, and differ in the various areas of their life. Emily and Bob can start working towards their vision tomorrow, but Emily hopes to reach her ultimate vision in a year, whilst Bob's target is 12 years.

Whether you have one goal in each area or twenty, you must fill in each of the 'W' columns for every goal that you come up with.

You will need to put plenty of time aside for this exercise. Enjoy it. Think about what it is you want out of life. Really go to town. I want to work on visions that you can make come true.

Now you have written down all of your life visions how has it made you feel?

Lists are great aren't they? Suddenly it as all there in black and white... or should I say blue?

**This is the blueprint, the game plan for your life.**

But this doesn't have to be it. This isn't carved in stone. It can be changed and added to as you continue on your project, as you travel on your journey. Just like a house can be altered and added to – so can your life. But at least now you have a definitive plan.

## Stage 2

As you look back on what you have written, take a closer look at the deadlines you have set yourself. What I would like you to do now with each and every one of your visions, is to decide upon the goal you want to set yourself for twelve months time, knowing that it will help you achieve your ultimate vision.

For example, Bob wants to have certain possessions by the age of forty, but what does he want to have achieved by the age of 29, in 12 months time, that will make him a step nearer to achieving his ultimate possession vision?

Bob needs to break down his 12 year vision into yearly goals and his yearly goals into monthly targets. That way Bob knows that he is moving a step forward to his ultimate vision as each month goes by.

**Remember; by the inch it's a cinch by the yard it's hard!**

You must do the same.

Right now how do you feel? Jubilant that you now have a defined game plan or exasperated at the amount of work that's involved.

I promise you this is worth every minute and every hour, every day and week that you put in. You will reap the benefits. You get out of life what you put in. This is my personal guarantee as your coach. As you begin to build towards your ultimate vision you will feel a sense of achievement and fulfilment that you may not have felt for a long time before, perhaps never.

Once you have your year-long goals, put them onto your chart and make sure you put it on the wall or in a workbook where you can view your game plan every day. Think about putting it on to the inside of your wardrobe door; turning it into a screensaver; pinning it by the mirror in the bathroom.

**Make sure you look at these visions daily and get excited about them. This is your life!**

## Stage 3

Beneath your year long goals, place your monthly targets. These, too, are critical.

At the end of every month you must take a look at what you have achieved. You must make sure you are moving in the right direction. If you haven't achieved them you must question yourself as to why this is the case. But at least you have an outcome – you know not what to do. Don't give up.

For example, if your health goal was to lose weight but you have gained five pounds, then you are clearly eating too much and not exercising enough – you know what to do! Don't give up!

Other reasons you may not have succeeded;

- Did you allow yourself enough dedicated time?
- Have you gone the extra mile?
- Did you use the resources available to you as you said you would?
- Do you still feel a strong desire and have a compelling reason to achieve your ultimate vision?

Ask yourself, 'what outcome have I produced that I can improve upon?' 'How can I make it better next time?'

Remember; persistance will overcome all resistance.

Because you have made all the right steps to getting your life in order, let's make sure that you have achieved your monthly targets. Tick them off the list – job done.

## How Do You Feel?

Remember those feelings when you first rode a bike, passed that exam, moved in to your first home... are you feeling those now?

Celebrate in a way that you see fit. Praise Your Game Now!

If you've lost 2 pounds towards your target of losing a stone - give yourself a treat of a glass of white wine.

If you've applied for that first career progression – well done. If you made the move, even better – take your partner out for a meal.

Share the news with your loved ones – especially those who want to see you do well and who will give you a pat on the back.

Remember; there is nothing wrong with seeking approval.

And...

**Never share your goals with the negative people, those who will pour water on your life goals. Only tell those who are going to support and cherish you.**

# My Last Word...

Now you are empowered with your personal game plan and you can build towards your vision for the future.

   You are working on making your life harmonious, balanced and more fulfilling. By working on your life's foundations and pillars, you will feel better and happier with your life. You are a player, and what a player!

   This is the start of an upward spiral.

   Remember; this day is the day you started to do something positive about your life. You are in the top 1% of achievers who are planning their ultimate vision. Well done! You are investing in your future.


**Love the Day!**